Julius Caesar, Charles Haines Keene

Tales of the Civil War

from Caesar's commentaries

Julius Caesar, Charles Haines Keene

Tales of the Civil War
from Caesar's commentaries

ISBN/EAN: 9783337409890

Printed in Europe, USA, Canada, Australia, Japan

Cover: Foto ©Andreas Hilbeck / pixelio.de

More available books at **www.hansebooks.com**

TALES OF THE CIVIL WAR

FROM

CAESAR'S COMMENTARIES.

ADAPTED FOR THE USE OF BEGINNERS

With Vocabulary, Notes, and Exercises

BY

CHARLES HAINES KEENE, M.A.

London

MACMILLAN AND CO.

AND NEW YORK

1894

CONTENTS.

INTRODUCTION.

THE three books of the Commentaries on the Civil War contain an account by Caesar himself of the contest between him and Pompey for the chief place in the Roman state. In the year 49 B.C., Pompey and Caesar were the two leading men of their time, and there was no independent authority competent to curb their rivalry. As neither could brook the superiority of the other, a conflict was inevitable, and their struggle for power involved their country in civil war.

Caesar begins his narrative by referring to a letter which he sent to the senate by the hands of Curio, in January, 49 B.C. In this letter it was proposed that both Pompey and Caesar should resign their provinces and disband their armies, and that Caesar should then go to Rome to stand for the consulship. The letter was read in the senate, but no resolution was moved upon it. A general discussion on the position of the state then took place, and finally a resolution was passed ordering Caesar to disband his army by a fixed day, under pain of being declared a public enemy. Hereupon the magistrates were armed with dictatorial power and preparations for war commenced. On learning this Caesar advanced to Ariminum, thereby leaving his province and practically declaring war against the senate. He rapidly took possession of a large number of towns in Italy, and so great was the alarm at Rome that the consuls fled to Capua. Domitius made a brief stand at Corfinium, but the town soon yielded to Caesar. Thereupon Pompey went to Brundisium, whither he was followed by Caesar, who began to block up the harbour. Pompey, however, succeeded in embarking his troops secretly, and crossed to Greece. Caesar through want of ships was unable to follow. He accordingly, abandoning the pursuit for the present, proceeded to Rome, where he summoned the senate and made an ineffectual attempt to treat with Pompey. He then went to Gaul and afterwards to Spain to conduct operations there, and he ultimately got the better of Pompey's supporters in both those countries.

In Africa, however, he was less fortunate, as his lieutenant, Curio, who had crossed thither from Sicily, was worsted and slain after an energetic campaign.

Caesar, during his absence from Rome, had been named dictator, and by virtue of that office on his return in 48 B.C. he took steps to restore credit and reestablish the public confidence which had been shaken by the war. Having carried out various measures with this view and presided over the elections, at which he was himself chosen one of the consuls, he resigned the dictatorship, and proceeding to Brundisium thence crossed to Greece. In the latter country the war was carried on with varying success for several months, until at last on August 9 (June 6 of the Julian calendar), 48 B.C., the two generals met on the field of Pharsalus. Here a decisive battle was fought in which Pompey was defeated and compelled to take to flight. He first escaped to Amphipolis and afterwards vainly sought safety at various places in Asia and the neighbouring islands. He finally determined to seek shelter in Egypt, but on attempting to land in that country he was treacherously slain by Achillas and Septimius, the advisers of the young king Ptolemy.

The present selections end with this tragic event, which practically left Caesar master of the Roman world. The few remaining chapters of the Commentaries describe the pursuit of Pompey, Caesar's arrival in Egypt and the commencement of the Alexandrine war.

The Tales here given are much abridged from the original, and the language has been somewhat simplified, especially in the earlier sections. The Exercises are based on the text, and it has not

been thought necessary to give an English-Latin
Vocabulary, as most of the words used in each
Exercise occur in the corresponding section of the
text, except in the case of some very common
words and of a few others which are supplied within
brackets in the several Exercises.

The Vocabulary is divided into sections corresponding with those of the text, and each Latin
word is explained in the Vocabulary on its first
occurrence. When the same word recurs in a later
part of the book its place in the Vocabulary may
be found by means of the Index.

The Notes supplement the Vocabulary in the few
cases where an explanation of the text is required
in a form not suitable for a Vocabulary.

In preparing the Text and Notes I am chiefly
indebted to Kraner and Hofmann's edition of the
three books of the Commentaries. I have also de-
rived some assistance from Malcolm Montgomrey's
excellent edition of the first book.

PART OF
ITALY

Roman Miles
0   25   50   100

English Miles
0   25   50   100

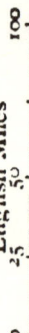

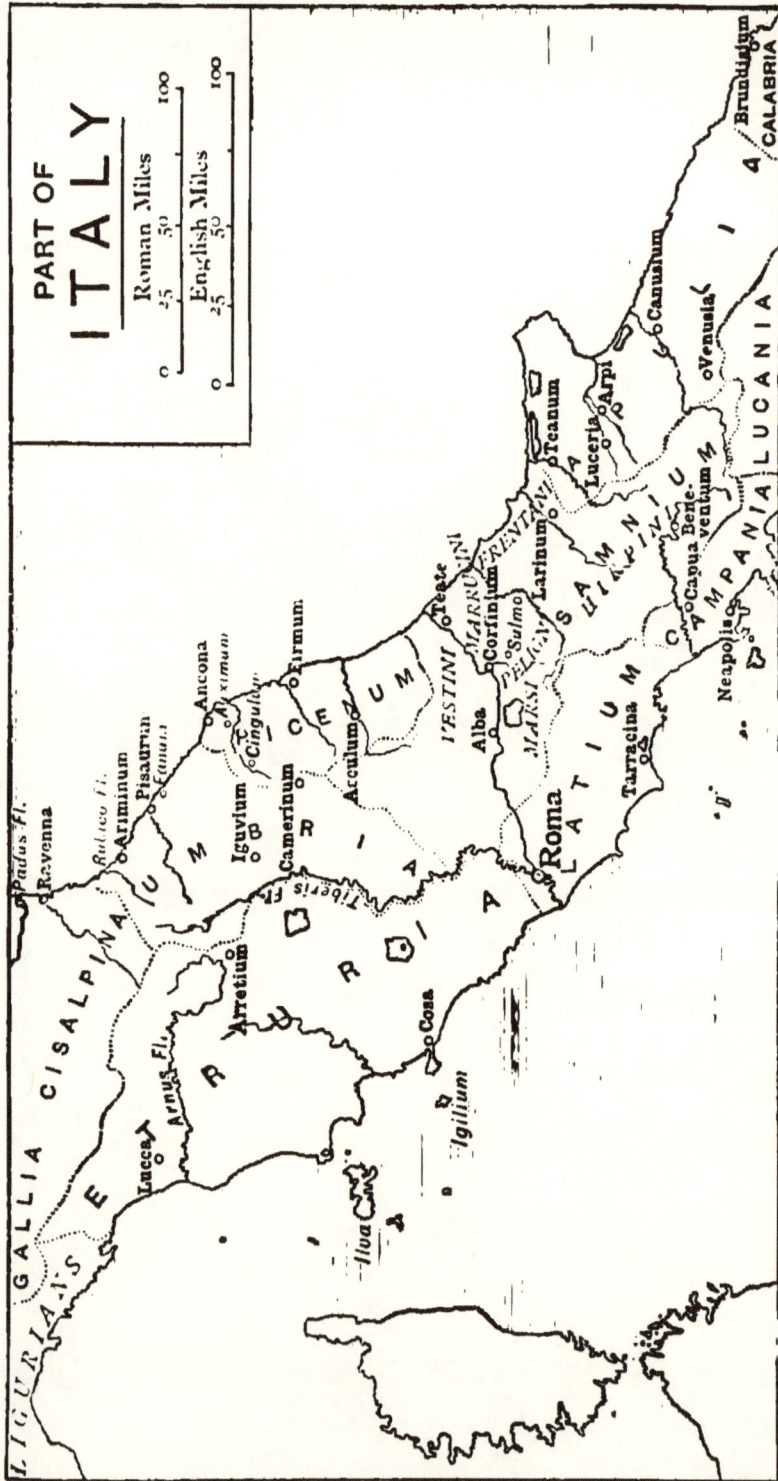

Walker & Boutall sc.

GALLIA CISALPINA

LIGURIA

Padus Fl.
Ravenna
Rubico Fl.
Ariminum
Pisaurum
Ancona

UMBRIA

Arnus Flu.
Luca
Arretium

ETRURIA

Iguvium
Cingulum
Camerinum

Tiberis Fl.

PICENUM

Firmum

Asculum

Cosa

Igilium

Ilva

Tiferno

Teate
VESTINI
MARRUCINI
FRENTANI
Alba
Corfinium
Sulmo
PELIGNI
MARSI

Larinum
Teanum

SAMNIUM
HIRPINI

Luceria
Arpi

Canusium

Venusia

Roma
LATIUM

Tarracina

Capua
Bene-
ventum

Neapolis

CAMPANIA
LUCANIA

Brundusium
CALABRIA

TALES OF THE CIVIL WAR.

1. *A Letter from Caesar is read in the Senate and unfavourably received.*

Litterae a C. Caesare consulibus redduntur.

Aegre impetratum est ut in senatu recitarentur.

Referunt consules de republica infinite.

L. Lentulus consul senatui reique publicae se non defuturum pollicetur.

In eandem sententiam loquitur Scipio.

Dicit Pompeio esse in animo reipublicae non deesse.

Haec Scipionis oratio, quod senatus in urbe habebatur Pompeiusque aberat, ex ipsius ore Pompei mitti videbatur.

2. *Pompey prepares for War.*

Missus est ad vesperum senatus.

Omnes, qui sunt eius ordinis, a Pompeio evocantur.

Laudat eos Pompeius atque in posterum confirmat.

Completur urbs tribunis, centurionibus, evocatis.

Necessarii Pompei atque Caesaris inimici in senatum coguntur.

3

Horum vocibus et concursu terrentur infirmiores, dubii confirmantur, plerisque vero libere decernendi potestas eripitur.

✓ **3.** *The Senate arms the Magistrates with dictatorial power The Tribunes escape to Caesar.*

Iam Pompeius totum se ab Caesaris amicitia averterat et cum communibus inimicis in gratiam redierat.

Rem ad arma deduci studebat.

His de causis aguntur omnia raptim atque turbate.

Decurritur ad illud extremum atque ultimum senatusconsultum ;

Dent operam consules, praetores, tribuni plebis, ne quid respublica detrimenti capiat.

Profugiunt statim ex urbe tribuni plebis seseque ad Caesarem conferunt.

Is eo tempore erat Ravennae .exspectabatque suis lenissimis postulatis responsa.

✓ **4.** *Troops are levied in Italy. Caesar appeals to his Soldiers, who promise to support him.*

Proximis diebus habetur extra urbem senatus.

Pompeius eadem illa, quae per Scipionem ostenderat, agit.

Tota Italia dilectus habentur, arma imperantur, pecuniae a municipiis exiguntur, e fanis tolluntur.

Quibus rebus cognitis Caesar apud milites contionatur.

Iniurias inimicorum in se commemorat.
Conclamant legionis tertiae decimae, quae aderat, milites, sese paratos esse imperatoris sui iniurias defendere.

5. *Caesar leaves his Province and enters Italy.*

Cognita militum voluntate Caesar Ariminum cum ea legione proficiscitur.

Reliquas legiones ex hibernis evocat et subsequi iubet.

Ab Arimino M. Antonium cum cohortibus quinque Arretium mittit.

Ipse Arimini cum duabus subsistit ibique dilectum habere instituit.

Pisaurum, Fanum, Anconam singulis cohortibus occupat.

6. *Panic at Rome. The Consuls fly to Capua.*

Quibus rebus Romam nuntiatis tantus repente terror invasit ut Lentulus consul ex urbe profugeret.

Hunc Marcellus collega et plerique magistratus consecuti sunt.

Cn. Pompeius pridie eius diei ex urbe profectus iter ad legiones habebat, quas a Caesare acceptas in Apulia hibernorum causa disposuerat.

Nihil citra Capuam tutum esse omnibus videtur.

Capuae primum sese confirmant et colligunt.

B

7. *Caesar occupies Asculum and advances on Corfinium.*

Interea Caesar Asculum Picenum proficiscitur.

Id oppidum Lentulus Spinther decem cohortibus tenebat.

Qui Caesaris adventu cognito profugit, et in itinere in Vibullium Rufum missum a Pompeio incidit.

Vibullius milites ab eo accipit, ipsum dimittit et ad Domitium Ahenobarbum Corfinium magnis itineribus pervenit.

Caesarem adesse cum legionibus duabus nuntiat.

Caesar ipse unum diem rei frumentariae causa moratus Corfinium contendit.

Eo cum venisset ad oppidum constitit iuxtaque murum castra posuit.

8. *Domitius in vain seeks Help from Pompey. Corfinium surrenders to Caesar.*

Domitius ad Pompeium in Apuliam peritos regionum cum litteris mittit, qui petant atque orent, ut sibi subveniat.

Pompeius rescripsit, sese rem in summum periculum deducturum non esse.

Domitium ad se cum omnibus copiis venire iussit.

Id ne fieri posset, obsidione atque oppidi circummunitione fiebat.

Domitius arcano cum paucis familiaribus suis colloquitur consiliumque fugae capere constituit.

Divulgato Domitii consilio milites suae salutis
rationem habent.

Itaque legatos ex suo numero ad Caesarem mittunt:
sese paratos esse portas aperire et L. Domitium vivum
in eius potestatem tradere.

Caesar omnes senatores senatorumque liberos,
tribunos militum equitesque Romanos ad se produci
iubet.

Hos omnes dimittit incolumes.

Milites Domitianos sacramentum apud se dicere
iubet.

Eo die castra movet et in Apuliam pervenit.

9. *Pompey goes to Brundisium and thence secretly sails for
Greece.*

Pompeius his rebus cognitis, quae erant ad Corfinium gestae, Brundisium proficiscitur.

Consules Dyrrhachium cum magna parte exercitus
profecti sunt.

Pompeius cum viginti cohortibus Brundisii re-
manebat.

Caesar Brundisium pervenit et exitus administra-
tionesque Brundisini portus impedire instituit.

Pompeius, sive operibus Caesaris permotus sive
etiam quod ab initio Italia excedere constituerat,
milites silentio naves conscendere iubet, et sub
noctem naves solvit.

Caesar, etsi ad spem conficiendi negotii maxime probabat coactis navibus mare transire et Pompeium sequi, tamen eius rei moram temporisque longinquitatem timebat, quod omnibus coactis navibus Pompeius praesentem facultatem insequendi sui ademerat.

Itaque in praesentia Pompei sequendi rationem omittit, in Hispaniam proficisci constituit.

10. *Caesar assembles the Senate at Rome. Unsuccessful Attempt to treat with Pompey.*

Caesar milites in proxima municipia deducit; ipse ad urbem proficiscitur.

Coacto senatu iniurias inimicorum commemorat.

Patientiam proponit suam, cum de exercitibus dimittendis ultro postulavisset.

Acerbitatem inimicorum docet, qui, quod ab altero postularent, in se recusarent.

Dicit legatos ad Pompeium de compositione mitti oportere.

Probat rem senatus de mittendis legatis; sed, qui mitterentur, non reperiebantur, maximeque timoris causa pro se quisque id munus legationis recusabat.

Pompeius enim discedens ab urbe in senatu dixerat, eodem se habiturum loco, qui Romae remansissent et qui in castris Caesaris fuissent.

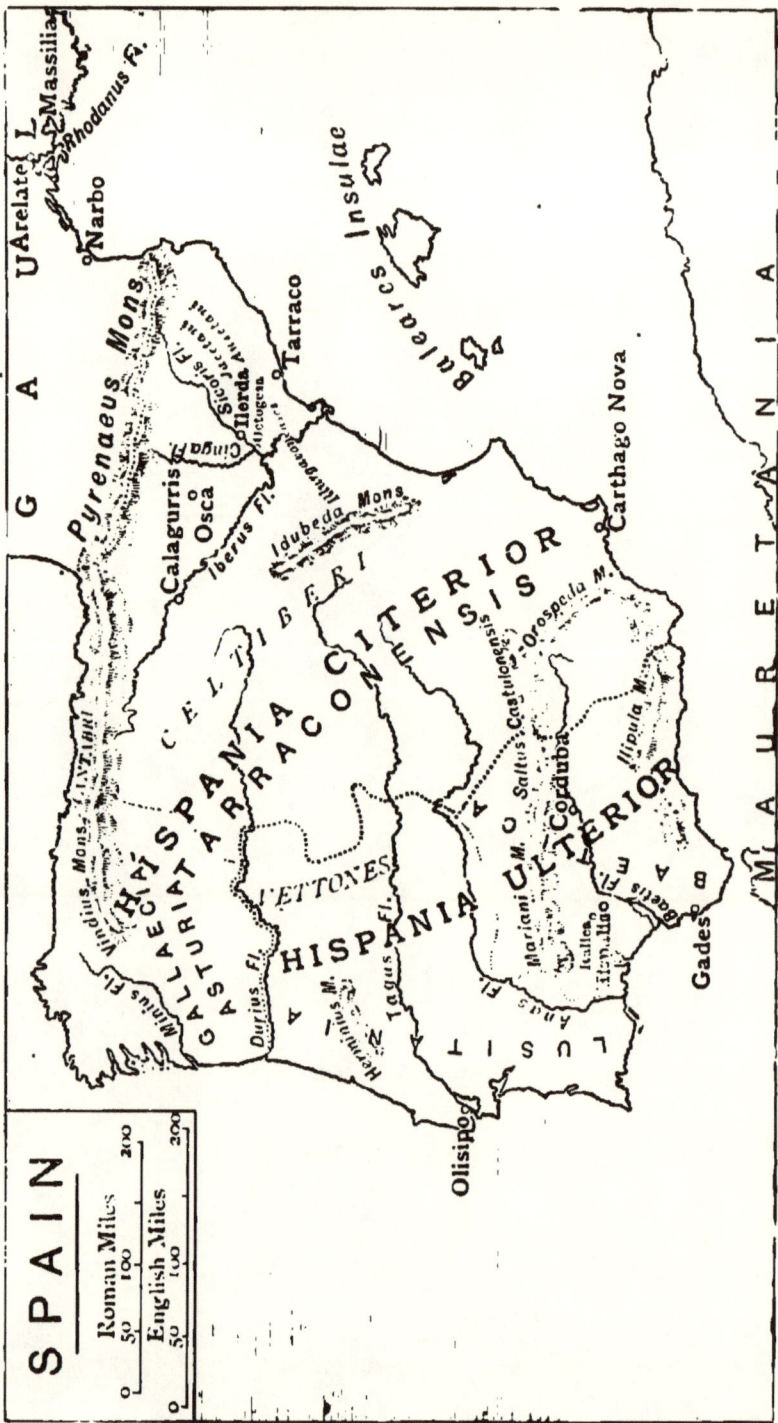

SPAIN

Roman Miles
50 100 200

English Miles
50 100 200

GALLIA

U Arelate L

Massilia

Rhodanus Fl.

Narbo

Pyrenaeus Mons

Tarraco

Baliares Insulae

Sicoris Fl.

Ilerda

Iluctogesa

Cinga

Calagurris

Osca

Iberus Fl.

Idubeda Mons

Carthago Nova

CELTIBERI

HISPANIA CITERIOR TARRACONENSIS

Orospeda M.

LVITANI

Vindius Mons.

Minius Fl.

GALLAECIA

ASTURIA

HISPANIA

VETTONES

HISPANIA ULTERIOR

Mariani M.

Saltus Castulonensis

Corduba

Ilipula M.

Baetis Fl.

Durius Fl.

Herminius M.

Tagus Fl.

HISPANIA

LUSIT

Anas Fl.

Ilipa M.

Hispalis

Italica

Gades

Olisipo

MAURETANIA

Walk. & Boutall sc.

Itaque Caesar frustra diebus aliquot consumptis ab urbe proficiscitur atque in ulteriorem Galliam pervenit.

11. *Pompey's Lieutenants prepare to hold Spain.*

C. Fabium legatum cum legionibus tribus in Hispaniam praemittit celeriterque saltus Pyrenaeos occupari iubet, qui eo tempore ab L. Afranio legato praesidiis tenebantur.

Afranius et Petreius et Varro legati Pompei erant. Horum unus Hispaniam citeriorem tribus legionibus, alter ulteriorem a saltu Castulonensi ad Anam duabus legionibus, tertius ab Ana Vettonum agrum Lusitaniamque pari numero legionum obtinebat.

Officia inter se partiuntur. Petreius ex Lusitania per Vettones cum omnibus copiis ad Afranium proficiscitur; Varro cum iis, quas habebat, legionibus omnem ulteriorem Hispaniam tuetur.

12. *Caesar appears before Ilerda and begins Operations.*

Fabius in Sicori flumine pontes effecerat duos distantes inter se milia passuum quattuor.

Eo Caesar cum equitibus nongentis pervenit.

Postero die triplici instructa acie ad Ilerdam proficiscitur et sub castris Afranii consistit.

Inter oppidum Ilerdam et proximum collem, ubi castra Petreius atque Afranius habebant, tumulus erat paulo editior.

Hunc si occupavisset Caesar et communisset, ab oppido et commeatu omni se interclusurum adversarios confidebat.

13. *Skirmish for possession of a Hill.*

Hoc sperans, legiones tres ex castris educit et unius legionis antesignanos procurrere atque eum tumulum occupare iubet.

Afranii cohortes breviore itinere ad eundem occupandum locum mittuntur.

Contenditur proelio et, quod prius in tumulum Afraniani venerant, nostri repelluntur atque terga vertere seque ad signa legionum recipere coguntur.

Caesar cohortatus suos legionem nonam subsidio ducit; hostem nostros insequentem supprimit rursusque terga vertere seque ad oppidum Ilerdam recipere et sub muro consistere cogit.

Haec eius diei praefertur opinio, ut se utrique superiores discessisse existimarent: Afraniani quod tumulum tenuissent, quae causa pugnandi fuerat, et nostros primo congressu terga vertere coegissent; nostri autem, quod iniquo loco congressi quinque horis proelium sustinuissent et adversarios in oppidum compulissent.

14. *Several Spanish Tribes join Caesar. Afranius and Petreius determine to retreat into Celtiberia.*

Interim Oscenses et Calagurritani mittunt ad Caesarem legatos seseque imperata facturos polli-

centur. Hos Tarraconenses et Iacetani et Ausetani
et paucis post diebus Illurgavonenses, qui flumen
Hiberum attingunt, insequuntur. Magna celeriter
commutatio rerum; multae longinquiores civitates ab
Afranio desciscunt et Caesaris amicitiam sequuntur.
Itaque constituunt Afranius Petreiusque in Celti-
beriam bellum transferre. Hic magnos equitatus
magnaque auxilia exspectabant et suis locis bellum
in hiemem ducere cogitabant. Hoc inito consilio
toto flumine Hibero naves conquirere et Octogesam
adduci iubent. Id erat oppidum positum ad Hiberum miliaque passuum a castris aberat triginta.
Ad eum locum fluminis navibus iunctis pontem im-
perant fieri legionesque duas flumen Sicorim traducunt.

15. *Caesar's Cavalry cross the Sicoris and harass the
Retreating Enemy.*

Caesar, qui partem aliquam Sicoris averterat
vadumque in eo flumine effecerat, huc iam reduxerat
rem, ut equites possent atque auderent flumen transire, pedites vero cum altitudine aquae tum etiam
rapiditate fluminis ad transeundum impedirentur.
Relinquebatur Caesari nihil, nisi uti equitatu agmen
adversariorum male haberet et carperet. Itaque
equites ab eo missi flumen transeunt, et cum de
tertia vigilia Petreius atque Afranius castra movis-
sent, repente sese ad novissimum agmen ostendunt
et iter impedire incipiunt.

γ 16. *Next day his Infantry also cross the River.*

Prima luce certior factus est Caesar, paratos esse milites ea transire flumen qua traductus esset equitatus. Etsi timebat tantae magnitudini fluminis exercitum obicere, conandum tamen atque experiendum iudicat. Itaque infirmiores milites ex omnibus centuriis deligi iubet, quorum aut animus aut vires videbantur sustinere non posse. Hos cum legione una praesidio castris relinquit; reliquas legiones expeditas educit magnoque numero iumentorum in flumine supra atque infra constituto traducit exercitum.

17. *Caesar overtakes the Enemy. Both Sides encamp and send out Reconnoitring Parties.*

Quos ubi Afranius conspexit, locis superioribus consistit aciemque instruit. Caesar in campis exercitum reficit, ne defessum proelio obiciat; rursus conantes progredi insequitur et moratur. Illi necessario maturius, quam constituerant, castra ponunt. Caesar quoque in proximo colle castra ponit.

Media circiter nocte fit certior Caesar, duces adversariorum silentio copias castris educere. Quo cognito signum dari iubet et vasa militari more conclamari. Illi exaudito clamore veriti, ne noctu impediti sub onere confligere cogerentur, iter supprimunt copiasque in castris continent.

Postero die Petreius occulte ad exploranda loca proficiscitur. Hoc idem fit ex castris Caesaris: mittitur L. Decidius Saxa, qui loci naturam perspiciat. Uterque idem suis renuntiat: quinque milia passuum proxima intercedere itineris campestris, inde excipere loca aspera et montuosa: qui prior has angustias occupaverit, ab hoc hostem prohiberi nihil esse negotii.

18. *Caesar makes a Detour over rough ground and by securing a Defile leading to the Ebro cuts the Enemy off from the River.*

Caesar omnes copias castris educit magnoque circuitu nullo certo itinere exercitum ducit. Nam quae itinera ad Hiberum atque Octogesam pertinebant, castris hostium oppositis tenebantur. Ac primo Afraniani milites visendi causa laeti ex castris procurrebant contumeliosisque vocibus prosequebantur nostros. Erat enim iter a proposito diversum, contrariamque in partem iri videbatur.

Sed ubi paulatim retorqueri agmen ad dextram conspexerunt iamque primos superare regionem castrorum animum adverterunt, conclamatur ad arma, atque omnes copiae exeunt rectoque ad Hiberum itinere contendunt. Erat in celeritate omne positum certamen, utri prius angustias montesque occuparent. Confecit prior iter Caesar atque ex magnis rupibus nactus planitiem in hac contra hostem aciem instruit.

Afranius, cum ante se hostem videret, collem quendam nactus ibi constitit.

19. *Afranius surrenders after making an Unsuccessful Attempt to return to Ilerda.*

Erat occasio bene gerendae rei. Sed Caesar in eam spem venerat, se sine pugna et sine vulnere suorum rem conficere posse, quod re frumentaria adversarios interclusisset. Premebantur Afraniani pabulatione, aquabantur aegre. Itaque magnus eorum cotidie numerus ad Caesarem perfugiebat. In his erat angustiis res. Sed ex propositis consiliis duobus explicitius videbatur Ilerdam reverti, quod ibi paulum frumenti reliquerant. Tarraco longius aberat; quo spatio plures rem posse casus recipere intellegebant.

Hoc probato consilio ex castris proficiscuntur. Caesar cum legionibus subsequitur. Pugnatur acriter ad novissimum agmen, compluresque milites interficiuntur. Tum vero consistunt necessario et procul ab aqua et natura iniquo loco castra ponunt. Tandem omnibus rebus obsessi, aquae, lignorum, frumenti inopia colloquium petunt. Venitur in eum locum quem Caesar delegit. Audiente utroque exercitu loquitur Afranius: Se perpessos omnium rerum inopiam; nunc vero neque corpore dolorem neque animo ignominiam ferre posse; itaque se victos confiteri. Ad ea Caesar respondit: Se nemini

nociturum. Provinciis excedere exercitumque di
mittere iussit.

20. *Varro at first wavers, but finally sides with Pompey.*

M. Varro in ulteriore Hispania initio cognitis iis
rebus, quae sunt in Italia gestae, diffidens Pompeianis
rebus, amicissime de Caesare loquebatur neque se in
ullam partem movebat. Postea vero, cum Caesarem
ad Massiliam detineri cognovit, copias Petrei cum
exercitu Afranii esse coniunctas, magna auxilia con-
venisse, atque haec ad eum latius atque inflatius
Afranius perscribebat, se quoque ad motus fortunae
movere coepit. Dilectum habuit tota provincia et
bellum parabat. Ratio autem haec erat belli, ut se
cum duabus legionibus Gades conferret, naves fru-
mentumque omne ibi contineret. Progresso ei paulo
longius litterae Gadibus redduntur, consensisse Gadi-
tanos principes cum tribunis cohortium, quae essent
ibi in praesidio, ut urbem insulamque Caesari ser-
varent.

21. *He is deserted by one of his Legions and surrenders to
Caesar. Caesar arrives at Marseilles and learns that he
has been named Dictator.*

His cognitis rebus altera ex duabus legionibus ex
castris Varronis, adstante et inspectante ipso, signa
sustulit seseque Hispalim recepit. Quibus rebus per-
territus Varro, cum itinere converso sese Italicam

venturum praemisisset, certior ab suis factus est praeclusas esse portas. Tum vero omni interclusus itinere ad Caesarem mittit, paratum se esse legionem, cui iusserit, tradere. Ille ad eum Sextum Caesarem mittit atque huic tradi iubet.

Caesar, qui magistratus principesque omnium civitatum sibi esse praesto iusserat, contione habita omnibus gratias agit, biduumque Cordubae commoratus Gades proficiscitur. Provinciae Q. Cassium praeficit. Ipse Tarraconem et inde Narbonem atque Massiliam pervenit. Ibi legem de dictatore latam seseque dictatorem dictum a M. Lepido praetore cognoscit.

22. *Surrender of Marseilles.*

Dum haec in Hispania geruntur, C. Trebonius legatus, qui ad oppugnationem Massiliae relictus erat, duabus ex partibus aggerem, vineas turresque ad oppidum agere instituit. Sed tanti erant antiquitus in oppido omnium rerum ad bellum apparatus tantaque multitudo tormentorum, ut eorum vim nullae contextae viminibus vineae sustinere possent. Tandem autem Massilienses omnibus defessi malis, rei frumentariae ad summam inopiam adducti, bis proelio navali superati, crebris eruptionibus fusi, gravi etiam pestilentia conflictati, sese dedere constituunt. Sed paucis ante diebus L. Domitius cognita Massiliensium voluntate naves tres comparav-

Sicilia

Walker & Boutall sc.

Prom. Mercurii

Anguillaria
Clypea
Cossyra

Hadrumetum
Thapsus

Sinus Carthaginiensis

Carthago
Sinus Carthaginiensis

Hippo Zarytus

Utica

Bagradas

Thenae

Syrtis Minor

Meninx

FIRST

ROMAN

PROVINCE

Zama

Tabraca

Guadianum Prom.

A F R I C A

R O M A N A

Hippo Regius

Sicca

L. Tritonia

Tretum Prom.

Cirta

N u m i d i a

Lambaesis

Sinus
Numidicus

Nasawath

M A U R E T A N I A

(Caesariensis)

Icosium

Chylemath

erat. Ex quibus unam conscendit et nactus turbidam tempestatem profectus est auxilioque tempestatis ex conspectu abiit. Massilienses arma tormentaque ex oppido proferunt, pecuniam ex publico tradunt. Caesar duas ibi legiones praesidio relinquit; ipse ad urbem proficiscitur.

23. *Curio's Campaign in Africa.*

Isdem temporibus C. Curio in Africam profectus ex Sicilia appellit ad eum locum, qui appellatur Anquillaria. Obsidere Uticam valloque circummunire instituit. Erat in oppido multitudo insolens belli diuturnitate otii. Itaque de deditione omnes iam palam loquebantur. Haec cum agerentur, nuntii praemissi ab rege Iuba venerunt, qui eum adesse cum magnis copiis dicerent et de custodia ac defensione urbis hortarentur. Huic simultas cum Curione intercedebat, quod tribunus plebis legem promulgaverat, qua lege regnum Iubae publicaverat.

Ex perfugis quibusdam audit Curio Iubam revocatum finitimo bello restitisse in regno, Saburram, eius praefectum, cum mediocribus copiis missum Uticae appropinquare. His auctoribus temere credens proelio rem committere constituit. Equitatum omnem prima nocte ad castra hostium mittit ad flumen Bagradam, quibus praeerat Saburra. Equites missi nocte imprudentes atque inopinantes Numidas aggrediuntur et magnum eorum numerum interficiunt.

c

24. *Battle at the River Bagrada.*

Curio cum omnibus copiis quarta vigilia exierat. Progressus milia passuum sex equites convenit, rem gestam cognovit. Equites sequi iubet sese iterque accelerat. At illi itinere totius noctis confecti subsequi non poterant, atque alii alio loco resistebant. Iuba certior factus a Saburra de nocturno proelio duo milia equitum, et peditum eam partem, cui maxime confidebat, Saburrae submittit; ipse cum reliquis copiis elephantisque sexaginta lentius subsequitur.

Saburra copias equitum peditumque instruit atque his imperat, ut simulatione timoris paulatim cedant ac pedem referant. Curio hostes fugere arbitratus copias ex locis superioribus in campum deducit. Dat suis signum Saburra, aciem constituit et circumire ordines atque hortari incipit. Non deest negotio Curio suosque hortatur. Ne militibus quidem ut defessis, neque equitibus, ut paucis et labore confectis, studium ad pugnandum virtusque deerat; sed hi erant numero ducenti, reliqui in itinere substiterant.

25. *Defeat and Death of Curio. A few of his Troops escape to Sicily. The rest surrender, of whom many are put to death by Juba.*

Hostium copiae submissis ab rege auxiliis crebro augebantur; nostros vires lassitudine deficiebant, simul ii, qui vulnera acceperant, neque acie excedere neque in locum tutum referri poterant, quod tota

acies equitatu hostium circumdata tenebatur. Hortatur Curionem Cn. Domitius, praefectus equitum, ut
fuga salutem petat atque in castra contendat. At
Curio numquam se amisso exercitu in Caesaris
conspectum reversurum confirmat atque ita proelians
interficitur. Equites ex proelio perpauci se recipiunt.
Milites ad unum omnes interficiuntur.

His rebus cognitis Marcius Rufus quaestor in castris
relictus a Curione cohortatur suos, ne animo deficiant.
Illi orant atque obsecrant, ut in Siciliam navibus
reportentur. Pauci lenunculi ad officium imperiumque
conveniebant. Sed tanta erat completis litoribus
contentio, qui potissimum ex magno numero con-
scenderent, ut multitudine atque onere nonnulli
deprimerentur, reliqui hoc timore propius adire tardarentur. Quibus rebus accidit ut pauci milites in
Siciliam incolumes pervenirent.

Reliquae copiae missis ad Varum noctu legatorum
numero centurionibus sese ei dediderunt. Quarum
cohortium milites postero die ante oppidum Iuba
conspicatus suam esse praedicans praedam magnam
partem eorum interfici iussit, paucos electos in regnum
remisit. Ipse diebus post paucis se in regnum cum
omnibus copiis recepit.

26. *Caesar's First Dictatorship.*

Dictator habet comitia Caesar, consules creantur
Iulius Caesar et P. Servilius. Cum fides tota Italia

esset angustior neque creditae pecuniae solverentur, constituit, ut per arbitros fierent aestimationes possessionum et rerum, quanti quaeque earum ante bellum fuisset, atque eae creditoribus traderentur. Hoc et ad timorem novarum tabularum tollendum minuendumque, qui fere bella et civiles dissensiones sequi consuevit, et ad debitorum tuendam existimationem esse aptissimum existimavit. Itemque nonnullos ambitus Pompeia lege damnatos illis temporibus, quibus in urbe praesidia legionum Pompeius habuerat, in integrum restituit. His rebus et feriis Latinis comitiisque omnibus perficiendis undecim dies tribuit dictaturaque se abdicat et ab urbe proficiscitur Brundisiumque pervenit.

27. *Caesar crosses to Greece with a part of his Troops.*

Eo legiones duodecim, equitatum omnem venire iusserat. Sed tantum navium repperit, ut anguste quindecim milia legionariorum militum, sexcenti equites transportari possent. Hoc unum Caesari ad celeritatem conficiendi belli defuit. Pompeius annuum spatium ad comparandas copias nactus, quod vacuum a bello atque ab hoste otiosum fuerat, magnam classem coegerat, legiones effecerat civium Romanorum novem, frumenti vim maximam comparaverat. Hiemare Dyrrhachii, Apolloniae omnibusque oppidis maritimis constituerat, ut mare transire Caesarem prohiberet, eiusque rei causa omni

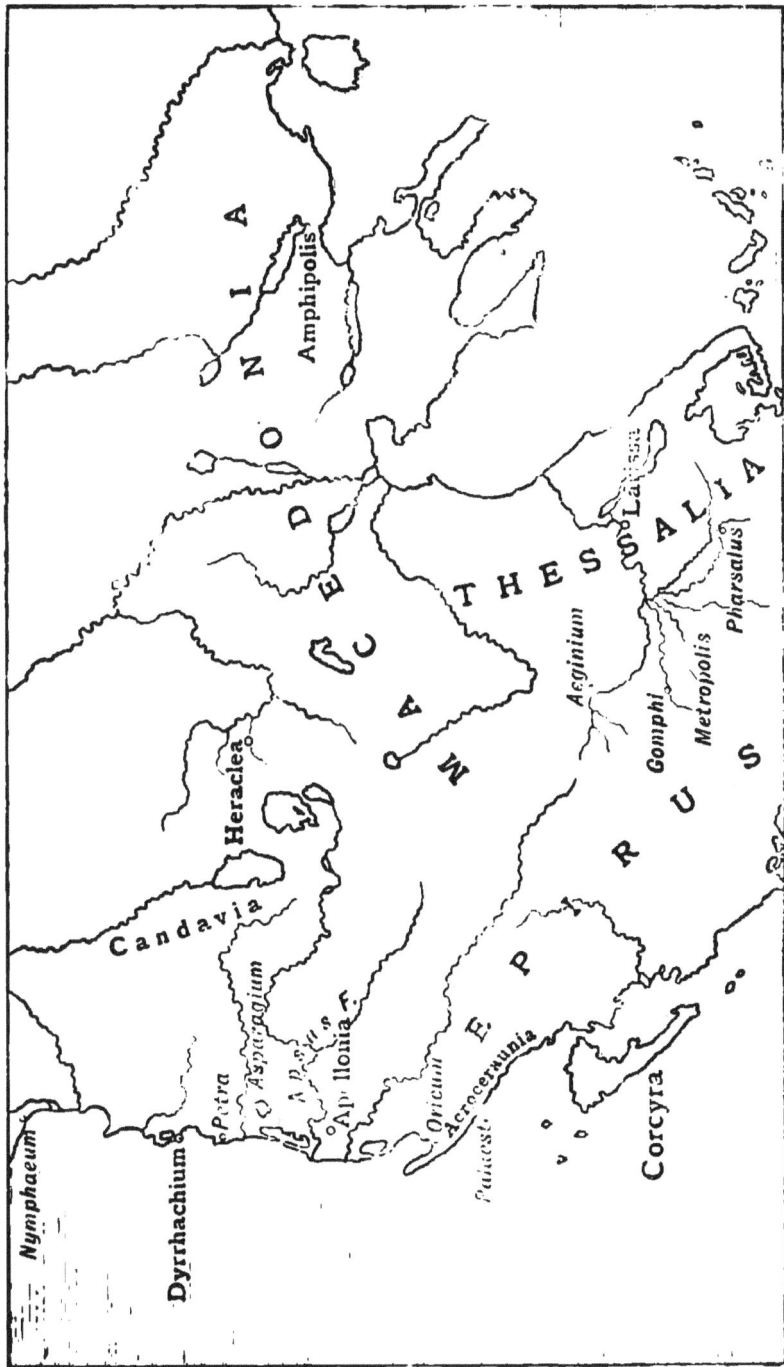

Walker & Boutall sc.

Nymphaeum

Dyrrhachium

Candavia

Heraclea

Petra

Asparagium

Apsus f.

Apollonia f.

Oricum

Acroceraunia

Palaeste

EPIRUS

Corcyra

MACEDONIA

Amphipolis

THESSALIA

Aeginium

Larissa

Gomphi

Metropolis

Pharsalus

ora maritima classem disposuerat. Caesar, ut
Brundisium venit, contionatus apud milites, con-
clamantibus omnibus, quodcumque imperavisset, se
aequo animo esse facturos, naves solvit. Postridie
terram attigit Cerauniorum saxa inter et alia loca
periculosa quietam nactus stationem, et ad eum
locum, qui appellabatur Palaeste, omnibus navibus
ad unam incolumibus milites exposuit.

28. *He sends back his Ships for the rest of the Troops, but
Bibulus meets and destroys many of them on the passage.*

Expositis militibus naves eadem nocte Brundisium
a Caesare remittuntur, ut reliquae legiones equitatus-
que transportari possent. Sed serius a terra pro-
vectae naves neque usae nocturna aura in redeundo
offenderunt. Bibulus enim Corcyrae certior factus
de adventu Caesaris inanibus occurrit, et nactus circiter triginta omnes incendit eodemque igne nautas
dominosque navium interfecit. Hoc confecto negotio
litora omnia longe lateque classibus occupavit.

29. *Unsuccessful Attempt of Octavius to seize Salonae for
Pompey.*

M. Octavius cum iis, quas habebat, navibus Salonas
pervenit: oppidum oppugnare instituit. Est autem
oppidum et loci natura et colle munitum. Sed cives
Romani, cum essent infirmi ad resistendum propter
paucitatem hominum, ad extremum auxilium descen-

derunt servosque omnes puberes liberaverunt. Octavius quinis castris oppidum circumdedit atque uno tempore obsidione et oppugnationibus eos premere coepit. Illi nacti occasionem meridiani temporis in proxima Octavii castra irruperunt et Octavium in naves confugere coegerunt. Iamque hiems appropinquabat et Octavius desperata oppugnatione oppidi Dyrrhachium sese ad Pompeium recepit.

30. *Caesar again attempts to treat with Pompey. Oricum and Apollonia open their Gates to Caesar.*

L. Vibullium Rufum, Pompei praefectum, pro suis beneficiis Caesar idoneum iudicaverat, quem cum mandatis ad Cn. Pompeium mitteret, eundemque apud Cn. Pompeium auctoritatem habere intellegebat. Vibullius ad Pompeium contendit, ut adesse Caesarem nuntiaret. Pompeius erat eo tempore in Candavia iterque ex Macedonia in hiberna Apolloniam Dyrrhachiumque habebat. Sed re nova perturbatus maioribus itineribus Apolloniam petere coepit, ne Caesar orae maritimae civitates occuparet. At ille expositis militibus eodem die Oricum proficiscitur. Quo cum venisset, L. Torquatus, qui iussu Pompei oppido praeerat, portas aperuit et se atque oppidum Caesari dedidit. Recepto Caesar Orico nulla interposita mora Apolloniam proficiscitur. Eius adventu audito Apolloniates ad Caesarem legatos mittunt oppidoque recipiunt.

31. *Caesar and Pompey encamp on opposite sides of the River Apsus.*

At Pompeius cognitis his rebus, quae erant Orici atque Apolloniae gestae, Dyrrhachio timens, diurnis eo nocturnisque itineribus contendit. Simul Caesar appropinquare dicebatur. Sed cum prope Dyrrhachium Pompeius constitisset castraque metari iussisset, Caesar praeoccupato itinere ad Dyrrhachium finem properandi facit castraque ad flumen Apsum ponit in finibus Apollonatium. Ibi reliquarum ex Italia legionum adventum exspectare et sub pellibus hiemare constituit. Hoc idem Pompeius fecit et trans flumen Apsum positis castris eo copias omnes auxiliaque conduxit.

32. *Reinforcements from Italy land at Nymphaeum and succeed in joining Caesar.*

Multi iam menses erant et hiems praecipitaverat, neque Brundisio naves legionesque ad Caesarem veniebant. Ac nonnullae eius rei praetermissae occasiones Caesari videbantur. Quibus rebus permotus Caesar Brundisium ad suos severius scripsit, nacti idoneum ventum ne occasionem navigandi dimitterent. Illi administrantibus M. Antonio et Fufio Caleno nacti austrum naves solvunt atque altero die Apolloniam praetervehuntur. Nacti portum, qui appellatur Nymphaeum, eo naves introduxerunt.

Haec eodem fere tempore Caesar atque Pompeius cognoscunt. Diversa sibi ambo consilia capiunt: Caesar, ut quam primum se cum Antonio coniungeret; Pompeius, ut venientibus in itinere se opponeret, si imprudentes ex insidiis adoriri posset. Eodem die uterque eorum ex castris stativis a flumine Apso exercitum educunt, Pompeius clam et noctu, Caesar palam atque interdiu. Pompeius idoneum locum nactus, ibi copias collocavit suosque omnes castris continuit ignesque fieri prohibuit, quo occultior esset eius adventus. Haec ad Antonium statim per Graecos deferuntur. Ille missis ad Caesarem nuntiis unum diem sese castris tenuit; altero die ad eum pervenit Caesar. Cuius adventu cognito Pompeius, ne duobus circumcluderetur exercitibus, ex eo loco discedit omnibusque copiis ad Asparagium pervenit atque ibi idoneo loco castra ponit.

33. *Operations at Asparagium. Pompey is cut off from Dyrrhachium and encamps at Petra.*

Caesar, postquam Pompeium ad Asparagium esse cognovit, eodem cum exercitu profectus, tertio die ad Pompeium pervenit juxtaque eum castra posuit et postridie eductis omnibus copiis decernendi potestatem Pompeio fecit. Ubi illum suis locis se tenere animum advertit, aliud sibi consilium capiendum existimavit. Itaque postero die magno circuitu difficili angustoque itinere Dyrrhachium profectus est,

sperans Pompeium aut Dyrrhachium compelli aut ab
eo intercludi posse, quod omnem commeatum eo con-
tulisset. Pompeius per exploratores certior factus
postero die castra movit, breviore itinere se occurrere
ei posse sperans. Quod fore suspicatus Caesar mili-
tesque adhortatus, ut aequo animo laborem ferrent,
parva parte noctis itinere intermisso mane Dyrrhachium venit, cum primum agmen Pompei procul cerne-
retur, atque ibi castra posuit. Pompeius interclusus
Dyrrhachio, edito loco, qui appellatur Petra aditumque
habet navibus mediocrem atque eas a quibusdam
protegit ventis, castra communit.

34. *Caesar changes his Plans and determines to effect a Junction
with Domitius in Macedonia. Pompey hastens in the same
Direction to support Scipio. Domitius narrowly escapes
falling into Pompey's hands and joins Caesar at Aeginium.*

Caesar a superioribus consiliis depulsus omnem sibi
commutandam belli rationem existimavit. Itaque
impedimenta omnia silentio prima nocte ex castris
Apolloniam praemisit, ipse de quarta vigilia proficiscitur. Neque vero Pompeius moram ullam ad in-
sequendum intulit. Caesari ad saucios deponendos
necesse erat adire Apolloniam. Sed timens Domitio,
ne adventu Pompei praeoccuparetur, ad eum omni
celeritate et studio incitatus ferebatur. Pompeius
quoque ad Scipionem properandum sibi existimabat;
si Caesar iter illo haberet, ut subsidium Scipioni

ferret; si ab ora maritima discedere nollet, quod legiones ex Italia exspectaret, ipse ut omnibus copiis Domitium aggrederetur. His de causis uterque eorum celeritati studebat. Sed Caesarem Apollonia a directo itinere averterat; Pompeius per Candaviam iter in Macedoniam expeditum habebat. Accessit etiam ex improviso aliud incommodum, quod Domitius, cum dies complures castris Scipionis castra collata habuisset, rei frumentariae causa ab eo discesserat et Heracliam, quae est subiecta Candaviae, iter fecerat, ut ipsa fortuna illum obicere Pompeio videretur. Sed Allobroges, qui ad Pompeium perfugerant, conspicati in itinere exploratores Domitii, Caesaris profectionem, adventum Pompei docuerunt. A quibus Domitius certior factus vix quattuor horarum spatio antecedens hostium beneficio periculum vitavit et ad Aeginium, quod est obiectum Thessaliae, Caesari venienti occurrit.

35. *Caesar takes Gomphi by storm. Metropolis and the other Cities of Thessaly except Larissa submit to him.*

Coniuncto exercitu Caesar Gomphos pervenit, quod est oppidum primum Thessaliae venientibus ab Epiro. Eodem, quo venerat, die post horam nonam oppidum altissimis moenibus oppugnare aggressus ante solis occasum expugnavit et ad diripiendum militibus concessit statimque ab oppido castra movit et Metropolim

venit. Metropolitae casu civitatis Gomphensis cognito portas aperuerunt. Quibus diligentissime con-
servatis, collata fortuna Metropolitum cum casu
Gomphensium, nulla Thessaliae fuit civitas praeter
Larisaeos, qui magnis exercitibus Scipionis tenebantur, quin Caesari parerent atque imperata facerent.
Ille idoneum locum in agris nactus plenis frumen-
torum, quae prope iam matura erant, ibi adventum
exspectare Pompei eoque omnem belli rationem conferre constituit.

36. *Pompey enters Thessaly. His Party are confident
of Victory.*

Pompeius paucis post diebus in Thessaliam pervenit
contionatusque apud cunctum exercitum suis agit
gratias, Scipionis milites cohortatur, receptisque omnibus in una castra legionibus suum cum Scipione
honorem partitur. Auctis copiis Pompei duobusque
magnis exercitibus coniunctis pristina omnium con-
firmatur opinio et spes victoriae augetur adeo ut, si
quando quid Pompeius tardius aut consideratius
faceret, unius esse negotium diei, sed illum delectari
imperio et consulares praetoriosque servorum habere
numero dicerent. Postremo omnes aut de honoribus
suis aut de praemiis pecuniae agebant neque quibus
rationibus superare possent, sed quemadmodum uti
victoria deberent cogitabant.

37. *Each side tries to secure Vantage Ground for a Battle.*

Re frumentaria praeparata confirmatisque militibus temptandum Caesar existimavit, quidnam Pompeius propositi aut voluntatis ad dimicandum haberet. Itaque ex castris exercitum eduxit aciemque instruxit. Pompeius, qui castra in colle habebat, ad infimas radices montis aciem instruebat, semper, ut videbatur, exspectans, si iniquis locis Caesar se subiceret. Caesar nulla ratione ad pugnam elici posse Pompeium existimans, hanc sibi commodissimam belli rationem iudicavit, uti castra ex eo loco moveret et insolitum ad laborem Pompei exercitum cotidianis itineribus defatigaret. His constitutis rebus, signo iam profectionis dato animum adversum est extra cotidianam consuetudinem longius a vallo esse aciem Pompei progressam, ut non iniquo loco posse dimicari videretur. Tunc Caesar apud suos, 'Differendum est,' inquit, 'iter in praesentia nobis et de proelio cogitandum. Animo simus ad dimicandum parati: non facile occasionem postea reperiemus'; confestimque expeditas copias educit.

38. *Battle of Pharsalia.*

Inter duas acies tantum erat relictum spatii, ut satis esset ad concursum utriusque exercitus. Sed

Pompeius suis praedixerat, ut Caesaris impetum exciperent neve se loco moverent aciemque eius distrahi paterentur. Sed nostri milites dato signo cum infestis pilis procucurrissent atque animum advertissent non concurri a Pompeianis, usu periti ac superioribus pugnis exercitati sua sponte cursum represserunt et ad medium fere spatium constiterunt, ne consumptis viribus appropinquarent, parvoque intermisso temporis spatio ac rursus renovato cursu pila miserunt celeriterque, ut erat praeceptum a Caesare, gladios strinxerunt. Neque vero Pompeiani huic rei defuerunt. Nam et tela missa exceperunt et impetum legionum tulerunt.

39. *Pompey's Cavalry at first gain some Advantage, but are afterwards routed and driven to the Mountains. General Rout of Pompey's Forces.*

Eodem tempore equites ab sinistro Pompei cornu universi procucurrerunt. Quorum impetum noster equitatus non tulit, sed paulatim loco motus cessit, equitesque Pompei aciem nostram a latere aperto circumire coeperunt. Quod ubi Caesar animum advertit, quartae aciei, quam instituerat sex cohortium, dedit signum. Illae celeriter procucurrerunt infestisque signis tanta vi in Pompei equites impetum fecerunt, ut eorum nemo consisteret omnesque con-

versi non solum loco excederent, sed protinus incitati
fuga montes altissimos peterent. Eodem impetu
cohortes sinistrum cornu pugnantibus etiam tum ac
resistentibus in acie Pompeianis circumierunt eosque
a tergo sunt adortae. Eodem tempore tertiam aciem
Caesar, quae quieta fuerat et se ad id tempus loco
tenuerat, procurrere iussit. Ita cum recentes atque
integri defessis successissent, alii autem a tergo adori-
rentur, sustinere Pompeiani non potuerunt atque
universi terga verterunt.

40. *Pompey retires to his Camp. The Camp is taken, and
Pompey, escaping with difficulty, makes his way first to
Larissa and afterwards to the Sea-shore where he embarks
on board a Corn Ship.*

Sed Pompeius, ut equitatum suum pulsum vidit
atque eam partem, cui maxime confidebat, perterritam
animum advertit, aliis quoque diffisus acie excessit
protinusque se in castra equo contulit, summae rei
diffidens et tamen eventum exspectans. Castra a
cohortibus, quae ibi praesidio erant relictae, industrie
defendebantur. Neque vero diu, qui in vallo con-
stiterant, multitudinem telorum sustinere potuerunt,
sed confecti vulneribus locum reliquerunt, protinusque
omnes ducibus usi centurionibus tribunisque militum
in altissimos montes, qui ad castra pertinebant, con-

fugerunt. Pompeius, iam cum intra vallum nostri
versarentur, equum nactus detractis insignibus imperatoris decumana porta se ex castris eiecit protinusque equo citato Larissam contendit. Neque ibi
constitit, sed eadem celeritate paucos suos ex fuga
nactus nocturno itinere ad mare pervenit navemque
frumentariam conscendit.

41. *Flight of Pompey.*

Caesar omnibus rebus relictis persequendum sibi
Pompeium existimavit, ne rursus copias comparare
alias et bellum renovare posset. Erat edictum Pompei
nomine Amphipoli propositum, uti omnes eius provinciae iuniores, Graeci civesque Romani, iurandi
causa convenirent. Sed utrum avertendae suspicionis
causa Pompeius proposuisset, ut quam diutissime
longioris fugae consilium occultaret, an novis dilecti-
bus, si nemo premeret, Macedoniam tenere conaretur,
existimari non poterat. Ipse ad ancoram una nocte
constitit et vocatis ad se Amphipoli hospitibus et
pecunia ad necessarios sumptus corrogata, cognito
Caesaris adventu ex eo loco discessit et Mytilenas
paucis diebus venit. Biduum tempestate retentus
navibusque aliis additis actuariis in Ciliciam atque inde Cyprum pervenit. Ibi cognoscit consensu omnium
Antiochensium civiumque Romanorum, qui illic nego-

D

tiarentur, arcem captam esse excludendi sui causa nuntiosque dimissos ad eos, qui se ex fuga in finitimas civitates recepisse dicerentur, ne Antiochiam adirent.

.

42. *Pompey arrives in Egypt and is there treacherously murdered.*

Quibus cognitis rebus, Pompeius, deposito adeundae Syriae consilio, aeris magno pondere ad militarem usum in naves imposito duobusque milibus hominum armatis Pelusium pervenit. Ibi casu rex erat Ptolemaeus, puer aetate, magnis copiis cum sorore Cleopatra bellum gerens, quam paucis ante mensibus per suos propinquos atque amicos regno expulerat; castraque Cleopatrae non longo spatio ab eius castris distabant. Ad eum Pompeius misit, ut pro hospitio atque amicitia patris Alexandria reciperetur atque illius opibus in calamitate tegeretur. Sed amici regis, qui propter aetatem eius in procuratione erant regni, sive timore adducti, ut postea praedicabant, sollicitato exercitu regio, ne Pompeius Alexandriam Aegyptumque occuparet, sive despecta eius fortuna, ut plerumque in calamitate ex amicis inimici existunt, iis, qui erant ab eo missi, palam liberaliter responderunt eumque ad regem venire iusserunt: ipsi clam consilio inito Achillam, praefectum regium, singulari homi-

nem audacia, et L. Septimium, tribunum militum, ad
interficiendum Pompeium miserunt.   Ab his liberaliter
ipse appellatus et quadam notitia Septimii productus,
quod bello praedonum apud eum ordinem duxerat,
naviculam parvulam conscendit cum paucis suis : ibi
ab Achilla et Septimio interficitur.

ABBREVIATIONS.

a., active.
abbrev., abbreviation.
abl., ablative.
abs., absolute.
acc., accusative.
adj., adjective.
adv., adverb.
com., common.
comp., comparative.
conj., conjunction.
contr., contraction.
dat., dative.
defect., defective.
dem., demonstrative.
distrib., distributive.
esp., especially.
f., feminine.
freq., frequentative.
fut., future.
gen., genitive.
gov., governing.
imperat., imperative.
impf., imperfect.
impers., impersonal.
incept., inceptive.
indecl., indeclinable.
indef., indefinite.
inf., infinitive.
interrog., interrogative.
irreg., irregular.

lit., literally.
m., masculine.
n., neuter.
n. f., noun feminine.
n. m., noun masculine.
n. n., noun neuter.
num., numeral.
part., participle.
part.adj., participial adjective.
pass., passive.
perf., perfect.
pers., person.
pl., plural.
poss., possessive.
prep., preposition.
pres., present.
pron., pronoun.
pronom., pronominal.
reflex., reflexive.
rel., relative.
sing., singular.
subj., subjunctive.
subst., substantive.
superl., superlative.
trans., transitive.
usu., usually.
v. a., verb active.
v. dep., verb deponent.
v. n., verb neuter.
voc., vocative.

VOCABULARY.

1.

lĭtter-a, -ae, n. f. sing., *a letter* (of the alphabet); pl., *a letter, epistle.*

a or **ab,** prep. gov. abl., *by, from, away.*

C., abbrev. for **Caius,** n. m., a praenomen.

Caes-ar, -ăris, n. m., *Caesar,* a cognomen.

cons-ul, -ŭlis, n. m., *consul,* one of the two supreme magistrates at Rome.

reddo, reddĭdi, reddĭtum, v. a. 3, *restore, deliver* (a letter).

aegrē, adv., *scarcely, with difficulty;* comp., **aegrius;** superl., **aegerrĭmē.**

impĕtro, v. a. 1, *obtain* (by asking).

sum, esse, fui, v. n. irreg., *am.*

ut or **utī,** conj. with subj., *that, so that, in order that;* adv., *as, how, when.*

in, prep. with acc., *into, for, against, to;* with abl., *in, on, at, upon, among.*

sěnāt-us, -ūs, n. m., *the senate,* the council of elders or nobles at Rome.

rěcĭto, v. a. 1, *read, read aloud.*

rěfěro, referre, rettŭli, relātum, v. a. irreg., *carry back, bear back, propose a motion;* **pedem referre,** *to retire, retreat.*

de, prep. gov. abl., *from, concerning, about, of the number of;* **his de causis,** *for these reasons;* **de tertia vigilia,** *in the third night-watch.*

respublica, reipublicae, n. f., *the state, the commonwealth.*

infīnĭtē, adv., *without limitation, in general terms* (as contrasted with a motion on some particular matter).

L., abbrev. for **Lucius,** a praenomen.

Lentul-us, -i, n. m., a cognomen.

-que, enclitic conj., *and.*

sui (there is no nom.), dat. **sibi;** acc. and abl. **se** or **sese,** pron. of 3rd pers. sing. and pl., *himself, herself, itself, themselves, he, she, it, they.*

33

non, adv., *not.*
desum, deesse, defui, v. n.
irreg., with dat., *fail, am
wanting;* defuturum (supply
esse), fut. inf.
polliceor, polliceri, pollicitus
sum, v. dep. a. and n. 2,
promise.
idem, eadem, idem, pron., *the
same.*
sententi-a, -ae, n. f., *opinion,
purport.*
loquor, loqui, locutus sum, v.
dep. 3, n. and a., *speak,
talk.*
Scipi-o, -onis, n. m., *Scipio,* a
cognomen.
dico, dixi, dictum, v. a. 3, *say;*
dictatorem dicere, *to name
a dictator;* sacramentum
dicere, *to take the oath of
allegiance.*
Pompeius, Pompei, n. m., a
Roman gentile name; Pom-
pei-us, -a, um, adj., *of* or
*belonging to Pompey, Pom-
peian.*
anim-us, -i, n. m., *mind, spirit.*
hic, haec, hoc, dem. pron.,
this.
orati-o, -onis, n. f., *speech.*
quod, conj., *because, that.*
urbs, urbis, n. f., *city,* esp. *the
city, Rome.*
habeo, habui, habitum, v. a. 2,
have, hold; senatum habere,
to hold a meeting of the senate.
absum, abesse, afui or abfui,
v. n. irreg., *am absent, am
distant.*
e or ex, prep. gov. abl., *from,
out of.*

ipse, ipsa, ipsum, gen. ipsius,
dem. pron. used both as subst.
and adj., *self, myself, himself,* etc.
os, oris, n. n., *mouth.*
mitto, misi, missum, v. a. 3,
*send, dismiss, utter, discharge,
hurl, launch, send word.*
video, vidi, visum, v. a. 2, *see;*
pass., *seem.*

2.

ad, prep. gov. acc., *to, at, near,
towards, for.*
vesp-er, -eris and eri, n. m.,
evening.
omn-is, -e, adj., *all, every.*
qui, quae, quod, gen. cuius,
rel. pron., *who, which, that.*
is, ea, id, gen. eius, dem. pron.,
he, she, it, that, this.
ord-o, -inis, n. m., *line, rank of
soldiers,class,order;* ordinem
ducere, *to command a company, be an officer, be a centurion.*
evoco, v. a. 1, *summon forth,
call out.*
laudo, v. a. 1, *praise.*
atque, conj., *and.*
poster-us, -a, -um, adj., *subse-
quent, next, ensuing;* in posterum (supply tempus), *for
the future.*
confirmo, v. a. 1, *strengthen,
encourage, reassure, assert,
protest;* se confirmare, *to
take courage.*
compleo, complevi, completum,
v. a. 2, *fill.*
tribun-us, -i, n. m., *tribune;*
tribunus plebis, *a tribune of*

VOCABULARY.

the *plebs*, one of ten annual magistrates, whose duty it was to defend the rights of the plebeians ; **tribunus militum**, *a military tribune*, an officer of high rank. Each legion had six of them.

centuri-o, -ōnis, n. m., *centurion*, the commander of a *centuria* or company, occupying a station below the *tribunus*.

evocatus, perf. part. of **evoco**, used as a subst., *a soldier of the reserve.*

necessari-us, -a, -um, adj., *necessary, needful ;* **necessarius** as a subst., m. *an intimate friend, kinsman.*

inimic-us, i, n. m., *a* (personal) *enemy.*

cōgo, cŏēgi, coactum, v. a. 3, *collect, assemble* (the regular word for calling together the senate), *compel.*

vox, vocis, n. f., *voice ;* in pl., *cries, expressions* (esp. of abuse).

et,conj.,*and;* **et** ..**et**,*both...and.*

concurs-us, -ūs, n. m., *a running together, rallying, encounter, onset.*

terreo, v. a. 2, *alarm, frighten.*

infirm-us, -a, -um, adj., *weak, wavering.*

dubi-us, -a, -um, adj., *doubtful, irresolute, undecided.*

plerique, pleraeque, pleraque (sing. rare), adj., *very many, most.*

vero, adv., *but, however, indeed, in truth.*

lībĕrē, adv., *freely.*

decerno, decrēvi, decrētum, v. a. 3, *decide, decree, fight.*

potest-as, -ātis, n. f., *power.*

ērĭpio,ērĭpĕre, ērĭpui, ēreptum, v. a. 3, *snatch, take away.*

3.

iam, adv., *now, already, by this time.*

tōt-us, -a, -um, gen. totius, dat. toti, adj., *the whole of, all, wholly.*

ămīcĭti-a, -ae, n. f., *friendship.*

āverto, averti, aversum, v. a. 3, *turn away, divert ;* se avertere, *to alienate oneself, be estranged.*

cum, prep. gov. abl., *with ;* conj., *when, since ;* **cum** ... **tum**, *both ... and.*

commun-is, -e, adj., *shared together, common.*

grāti-a, -ae, n. f., *favour, gratitude ;* in gratiam redire, *to be reconciled :* in pl., *thanks;* gratias agere, *give thanks.*

rĕdeo, rĕdīre, rĕdīvi or rĕdii, rĕdĭtum, v. n. 4, *go back, return.*

res, rei, n. f., *thing, matter, affair, property, effects.*

arm-a, -orum, n. n. pl., *arms, weapons.*

dēdūco, deduxi, deductum, v. a. 3, *lead, bring down ;* milites deducere, with in and acc., *to quarter soldiers in a place.*

stŭdeo, v. a. and n. 2, *am zealous, eager, attend to, strive after.*

caus-a, -ae, n. f., *cause, reason;*
in abl. sing. with gen., *on
account of, for the sake of,
for.*

ăgo, ēgi, actum, v. a. 3, *do, act,
urge, plead, discuss, push on,
carry forward.*

raptim, adv., *hastily.*

turbātē, adv., *confusedly.*

dēcurro, dēcurri and dēcŭ-
curri, dēcursum, v. n. 3, *run
down;* with **ad**, *have recourse
to.*

ille, illa, illud, dem. pron.,
that, he, she, it.

extrēm-us, -a, -um, adj., *last,
hindmost.*

ultĭm-us, -a, -um, adj., *final.*

consult-um, -i, n. n., *decree;*
senatus consultum, *decree of
the senate.*

do, dăre, dĕdi, dătum, v. a. 1,
give.

ŏpĕr-a, -ae, n. f., *work, service;*
dare operam, *to take heed,
look to it.*

praet-or, -ōris, n. m., *praetor,*
one of the higher magistrates
at Rome.

plebs, plēbis, n. f., *the populace,
commons.*

nē, conj., *lest, that not;* adv.,
ne ... quidem. *not even.*

quis, qua, quid, indef. pron.,
any, anyone, anything.

detrĭment-um, -i, n. n., *injury,
loss.*

căpio, căpĕre, cēpi, captum,
v. a. 3, *take, receive, get.*

prŏfŭgio, profŭgĕre, profŭgi,
v. n. 3, *take to flight, escape.*

statim, adv., *immediately.*

confĕro, conferre, contŭli, col-
lātum, v. a. irreg., *bring
together, collect, compare;* se
conferre, *to betake oneself.*

temp-us, -ŏris, n. n., *time.*

Ravenn-a, -ae, n. f., *Ravenna.*

exspecto, v. a. and n. 1, *await,
wait, expect, anticipate.*

su-us, -a, -um, poss. pron., *his,
her, its, their;* **sui** (supply
milites), *his men, his troops.*

len-is, -e, adj., *gentle, mild,
moderate.*

postulat-um, -i, n. n., *demand.*

respons-um, -i, n. n., *answer,
reply.*

4.

proxĭm-us, -a, -um, superl.
adj., *nearest, very near, next.*

di-es, -ēi, n. m., *sometimes* f.
in sing., *day.*

extra, prep. gov. acc., *outside
of.*

per, prep. gov. acc., *through,
by, by means of.*

ostendo, ostendi, ostensum and
ostentum, v. a. 3, *show, declare, express;* **se ostendere,**
to show oneself, appear.

Itali-a, -ae, n. f., *Italy.*

dilect-us, -ūs, n. m., *conscrip-
tion, levy* (of troops).

impĕro, v. a. and n. 1, *order,
command, levy* (supplies).

pecuni-a, -ae, n. f., *money;* pl.,
sums of money.

municipi-um, -i, n. n., *a free
town* (particularly in Italy).

exĭgo, exēgi, exactum, v. a. 3,
demand, exact.

fān-um, -i, n. n., *shrine, temple.*

tollo, sustuli, sublātum, v. a. irreg. 3, *take up, remove, carry away.*

cognosco, cognōvi, cognĭtum, v. a. 3, *know, learn, hear of.*

apud, prep. gov. acc., *at, in presence of, with.*

mīl-es, -ĭtis, n. m., *soldier.*

contionor, contionatus sum, v. dep. 1, *make a speech to an assembly.*

iniurĭ-a, -ae, n. f., *wrong.*

commemŏro, v. a. 1, *mention, recount.*

conclāmo, v. a. and n. 1, *shout together;* **vasa conclamare,** *to shout or give the signal, before breaking up, for packing, to give the order for decamping,* elliptical for, conclamare ut vasa colligantur; **conclamare ad arma,** *to call to arms.*

legi-o, -ōnis, n. f., *legion,* a division of the Roman army, varying in number of men at different periods. In Caesar's time the legion was usually 3000 or 3600 strong, though it theoretically contained nearly double that number of men.

tertĭ-us, -a, -um, num. adj., *third;* **tertius decimus,** *thirteenth.*

decim-us, -a, -um, num. adj., *tenth.*

adsum, adesse, adfui, v. n. irreg., *am present, am at hand.*

parat-us, -a, -um, part. adj., *prepared, ready.*

impĕrāt-or, -ōris, n. m., *commander-in-chief, general.*

dēfen-do, -di, -sum, v. a. 3, *defend, repel, avert.*

5.

volunt-as, -ātis, n. f., *wish, will, inclination.*

Arimĭn-um, -i, n. n., *Ariminum,* now Rimini, a town in Umbria.

proficiscor, proficisci, profectus sum, v. dep. 3, *set out.*

relĭqu-us, -a, -um, adj., *remaining.*

hĭbern-a, -ōrum (supply castra), n. n. pl., *winter-quarters.*

subsĕquor, subsequi, subsecutus, v. dep. 3, *follow close after.*

iubeo, iussi, iussum, v. a. 2, *order, command.*

M., abbrev. for **Marcus,** a praenomen.

Antoni-us, -i, n. m., *Antony.*

cohor-s, -tis, n. f., *cohort,* one of the divisions of a legion.

quinque, indecl. num. adj., *five.*

Arreti-um, -i, n. n., *Arretium,* now Arezzo, a town in Etruria.

du-o, -ae, -o, num. adj., *two.*

subsisto, substiti, v. n. 3, *stop, stay behind.*

ĭbi, adv., *there.*

instituo, institui, institutum, v. a. 3, *set up, arrange, form, establish, begin.*

Pisaur-um, -i, n. n., *now Pesaro,* a city of Umbria.

Fan-um, -i, n. n., now *Fano*,
a city in Umbria.

Ancon-a, -ae, n. f., *Ancona*, a
city in Picenum.

singul-i, -ae, -a, distrib. num.
adj., *one apiece, one each.*

occŭpo, v. a. 1, *seize, occupy.*

6.

Rom-a, -ae, n. f., *Rome.*

nuntio, v. a. 1, *report, announce.*

tant-us, -a, -um, adj., *so great,
such.*

repente, adv., *suddenly.*

terr-or, -ōris, n. m., *fright,
panic.*

invādo, invāsi, invāsum, v. a.
3, *attack, fall on.*

Marcell-us, -i, n. m., *Marcellus.*

collēg-a, -ae, n. m., *colleague.*

magistrāt-us, -ūs, n. m., *magistrate.*

consĕquor, consĕqui, consĕcūtus
sum, v. dep. 3, *follow.*

Cn., abbrev. for Cnaeus, a praenomen.

prīdĭē, adv., *on the day before;*
often followed by eius diei,
*on the day before this day,
the day before.*

iter, itinĕris, n. n., *road, journey, way, march;* iter habere,
to be on one's way.

accĭpio, accĭpĕre, accēpi, ac-
ceptum, v. a. 3, *receive.*

Apuli-a, -ae, n. f., a district in
lower Italy.

dispōno, dispŏsui, dispŏsĭtum,
v. a. 3, *set in different places,
station.*

nihil, n. n., indecl., *nothing.*

citrā, prep. gov. acc., *on this
side of.*

Capu-a, -ae, n. f., the chief city
of Campania.

tut-us, -a, -um, adj., *safe.*

primum, adv., *first;* quam
primum, *as soon as possible.*

collĭgo, collēgi, collectum, v.
a. 3, *collect, gather;* se colli-
gere, *to rally.*

7.

intereā, adv., *meanwhile.*

Ascul-um, -i, n. n., now Ascoli,
the capital of Picenum.

Picen-us, -a, -um, adj., *Picene,
of or belonging to Picenum.*

oppĭd-um, -i, n. n., *town.*

Spinth-er, -ēris, n. m., a cognomen.

decem, num. adj., *ten.*

teneo, tenui, tentum, v. a. 2, *hold.*

advent-us, -ūs, n. m., *approach,
arrival.*

Vibulli-us, -i, n. m., a Roman
gentile name.

Ruf-us, -i, n. m., a cognomen.

incĭdo, incĭdi, v. n. 3, with in
and acc., *fall in with.*

dimitto, dimisi, dimissum, v.
a. 3, *dismiss, send away,
disband, let slip, neglect.*

Domiti-us, -i, n. m., a Roman
gentile name.

Ahenobarb-us, -i, n. m., a cognomen.

Corfini-um, -i, n. n., chief town
of the Peligni.

magn-us, -a, -um, adj., *great,
large;* magnum iter, *a forced
march;* comp., maior; superl.,
maxĭmus.

pervĕnio, pervēni, perventnm, v. n. 4, *make one's way, come to, reach.*

un-us, -a, -um, gen. unīus, num. adj., *one.*

frumentari-us, -a, -um, adj., *belonging to corn;* **res frumentaria,** *corn supply, provisions, commissariat;* **navis frumentaria,** *a provision ship, store-ship.*

moror, morātus sum, v. dep. n. and a. 1, *delay.*

contendo, contendi, contentum, v. n. 3, *strive, fight, hasten.*

ĕō, adv., *thither.*

vĕnio, vēni, ventum, v. n. 4, *come.*

consisto, constĭti, constĭtum, v. n. 3, *stand, make a stand, am posted, halt.*

iuxtā, prep. gov. acc., *near.*

mur-us, -i, n. m., *wall.*

castr-a, -orum, n. n. pl., *camp.*

pōno, pósui, pŏsĭtum, v. a. 3, *place, pitch* (a camp).

8.

perīt-us, -a, -um, adj. with gen., *experienced in, acquainted with, skilled in, skilful.*

regi-o, -ōnis, n. f., *region, district.*

pĕto, petīvi and petii, petītum, v. a. 3, *seek, beg, make for* (a place).

oro, v. a. 1, *pray, entreat.*

subvĕnio, subvēni, subventum, v. n. 4, with dat., *aid, help.*

rescrībo, rescripsi, rescriptum, v. a. 3, *write back, answer.*

summ-us, -a, -um, superl. adj., *highest, utmost.*

perīcŭl-um, -i, n. n., *peril, risk, danger.*

copi-a, -ae, n. f., *supply, plenty;* pl., *forces, troops.*

fīo, fĭeri, factus sum, v. used as pass. of **facio,** *am made, effected, become.*

possum, posse, potui, v. n. irreg., *am able.*

obsĭdi-o, -ōnis, n. f., *siege, blockade.*

circummunīti-o, -ōnis, n. f., *a line of investment.*

arcāno, adv., *secretly.*

pauc-i, -ae, -a (sing. very rare), adj., *few.*

familiar-is, -e, adj., *intimate;* as subst. m., *intimate friend.*

collŏquor, collŏqui, collŏcutus sum, v. dep. 3, with **cum,** *converse with.*

consili-um, -i, n. n., *advice, plan.*

fug-a, -ae, n. f., *flight.*

constituo, constitui, constitū-tum, v. a. 3, *set, post, draw up, appoint, determine.*

divulgo, v. a. 1, *make commonly known, publish.*

sal-ūs, -ūtis, n. f., *safety.*

rati-o, -ōnis, n. f., *reason, plan, method;* **rationem habere** with gen., *to take account of, provide for.*

Ĭtăque, conj., *and so, therefore, accordingly.*

lēgāt-us, -i, n. m., *ambassador, envoy, lieutenant.*

numĕr-us, -i, n. m., *number, rank.*

port-a, -ae, n. f., *gate.*
aperio, aperui, apertum, v. a. 4, *open.*
viv-us, -a, -um, adj., *alive, living.*
trado, tradidi, traditum, v. a. 3, *hand over, deliver, surrender.*
senāt-or, -ōris, n. m., *senator,* a member of the Roman senate.
libĕr-i, -ōrum, n. m. pl., *children.*
eques, equĭtis, n. m., *horseman,* (Roman) *knight;* pl., *cavalry.*
Roman-us, -a, -um, adj., *of* or *belonging to Rome, Roman.*
prodūco, produxi, productum, v. a. 3, *lead* or *bring out, lead forward, induce.*
incolŭm-is, -e, adj., *unharmed, safe.*
Domitian-us, -a, -um, adj., *of* or *belonging to Domitius.*
sacrament-um, -i, n. n., *military oath of allegiance.*
mŏveo, mōvi, mōtum, v. a. 2, *more;* castra movere, *to break up camp.*

9.

gero, gessi, gestum, v. a. 3, *carry on, wage, administer;* in pass., *happen, take place, be done;* rem bene gerere, *to fight with success, to strike a decisive blow.*
Brundisi-um, -i, n. n., *Brundisium,* now Brindisi, a town in Calabria, the chief naval station of the Romans in

the Adriatic, and their regular point of departure for Greece.
Dyrrhachi-um, -i, n. n., *Dyrrhachium,* now Durazzo, a sea-coast town of Illyria, the chief landing-place of those coming from Italy to Greece.
pars, partis, n. f., *part, portion, party, side;* contrariam in partem, *in an opposite direction.*
exercĭt-us, -ūs, n. m., *army.*
viginti, num. adj., *twenty.*
remăneo, remansi, remansum, v. n. 2, *stay behind, remain.*
exĭt-us, -ūs, n. m., *going out, egress, outlet.*
administrati-o, -ōnis, n. f., *direction, management, the working* (of a harbour).
Brundisīn-us, -a, -um, adj., *of* or *belonging to Brundisium.*
port-us, -ūs, n. m., *harbour, port.*
impĕdio, impedivi or impedii, impedītum, v. a. 4, *hinder, obstruct, hamper.*
sive, conj., *or if;* sive ... sive, *whether ... or.*
opus, opĕris, n. n., *work;* pl., *siege works, fortifications.*
permŏveo, permōvi, permōtum, v. a. 2, *move greatly, alarm.*
etiam, conj., *even, also.*
initi-um, -i, n. n., *beginning;* the abl. initio is used as an adv., *in the beginning, at first.*

excēdo, excessi, excessum, v. n. 3, with abl., *go out from, quit*.

silenti-um, i, n. n., *silence*.

nav-is, -is, n. f., *vessel, ship*.

conscendo, conscendi, conscensum, v. a. and n. 3, *go on board, embark on*.

sub, prep. with acc., *up to, just before, towards;* with abl., *under, below, near, at the time of*.

nox, noctis, n. f., *night*.

solvo, solvi, solūtum, v. a. 3, *loosen, pay, discharge, pay off;* **navem solvere**, *weigh anchor, set sail*.

etsi, conj., *although*.

spes, spei, n. f., *hope*

conficio, conficĕre, confēci, confectum, v. a. 3, *make up, complete, finish, end, carry out, wear out;* **confectus**, *exhausted*.

negoti-um, -i, n. n., *business, difficulty*.

maximē, superl. adj., *chiefly, most, especially*.

proLo, v. a. 1, *approve*.

mărĕ, măris, n. n., *sea*.

transeo, transīre, transivi or transii, transĭtum, v. a. and n. 4, *cross, pass over, desert*.

sequor, sequi, secūtus sum, v. dep. 3, *follow, pursue*.

tamen, conj., *however, nevertheless, yet*.

mor-a, -ae, n. f., *delay*.

longinquĭt-as, -ātis, n. f., *length, duration*.

timeo, v. a. and n. 2. *fear*.

praesens, praesentis, adj., *present*.

facult-as, -ātis, n. f., *power, opportunity*.

insĕquor, insĕqui, insecūtus sum, v. dep. 3, *follow, pursue*.

adĭmo, adēmi, ademptum, v. a. 3, *take away*.

praesenti-a, -ae, n. f., *the present;* **in praesentia**, *for the present*.

omitto, omīsi, omissum, v. a. 3, *give up, abandon*.

Hispani-a, -ae, n. f., *Spain*.

10.

patienti-a, -ae, n. f., *forbearance, endurance*.

propōno, propōsui, propōsĭtum, v. a. 3, *set before (one), set forth, represent, propose*.

ultro, adv., *to the further side, beyond expectation, actually, voluntarily*.

postŭlo, v. a. 1, *demand*.

acerbĭt-as, -ātis, n. f., *bitterness, harshness, malignity*.

doceo, docui, doctum, v. a. 2, *teach, instruct, set forth, tell of*.

alter, altéra, altĕrum, adj., *the other (of two), one (of two), the second*.

recūso, v. a. 1, *refuse*.

compositi-o, -ōnis, n. f., *settlement, agreement*.

oportet, oportuit, impers. v. 2, *it behooves, it is becoming, one ought*.

sed, conj., *but*.

repĕrio, reppĕri, repertum, v. a. 4, *find*.

tim-or, -ōris, n. m. *fear, alarm.*

pro, prep. gov. abl., *before, in front of, on account of, in consideration of;* pro se quisque, *each for himself.*

quisque, quaeque, quodque, indef. pron., *each, every one.*

mun-us, -ōris, n. n., *duty, office.*

legati-o, -ōnis, n. f., *commission, embassy.*

enim, conj., *for.*

discēdo, discessi, discessum, v. n. 3, *depart, come off.*

loc-us, -i, n.m. (pl. loci, m. loca, n.), *place, spot, position;* eodem loco habere, *to hold in the same esteem.*

frustrā, adv., *in vain.*

aliquot, indecl. num. adj., *several.*

consūmo, consumpsi, consumptum, v. a. 3, *use up, consume, spend.*

ulteri-or, -us, gen. -ōris, comp. adj., *further;* Gallia ulterior, *Further* (that is, Transalpine) *Gaul;* Hispania ulterior, *Further Spain,* that is, Spain beyond the Ebro.

Galli-a, -ae, n. f., *Gaul.*

11.

Fabi-us, -i, n. m., a Roman gentile name.

tres, tria, trium, tribus, num. adj., *three.*

praemitto, praemīsi, praemissum, v. a. 3, *send forward, send in advance, send word beforehand.*

celerīter, adv., *quickly.*

salt-us, -ūs, n. m., *mountain-pass.*

Pyrenae-us, -a, -um, adj., *of or belonging to the Pyrenees, Pyrenaean.*

Afrani-us, -i, n. m., *Afranius,* a general of Pompey in Spain.

praesidi-um, -i, n. n., *defence, garrison.*

Petreius, Petrei, n. m., *Petreius,* a lieutenant of Pompey in the civil war.

Varr-o, -ōnis, n. m., *Varro,* a lieutenant of Pompey in the civil war, and a famous grammarian.

citeri-or, -us, gen. -ōris, comp. adj., *on this side;* Hispania citerior, *Hither Spain,* a name applied at first to the part of Spain north of the Ebro, but afterwards extended to the country as far south as the Saltus Castulonensis.

Castulonens-is, -e, adj., *of or belonging to Castulo,* a town in Hispania Tarraconensis, near the borders of Baetica, now the village of Cazlona; saltus Castulonensis, *the range of Castulo,* now the Sierra Morena.

Anas, Anae, n. m., *the Anas* (now the Guadiana), a river in Spain.

Vettōn-es, -um, n. m., pl., *the Vettones,* a people of Lusitania, in the modern Salamanca and Estremadura.

ager, agri, n. m., *land, territory.*

Lusitani-a, -ae, n. f., *Lusitania*, the western part of Spain, corresponding to the modern Portugal and part of the Spanish provinces of Estremadura and Toledo.

par, paris, adj., *equal*.

obtineo, obtinui, obtentum, v. a. 2, *hold, occupy*.

offici-um, -i, .n. m., *service, duty*.

inter, prep. gov. acc., *between, among*.

partior, partitus sum, v. dep. 4, *share, divide*.

tueor, tuitus sum, v. dep. 2, *defend, protect*.

12.

Sicor-is, -is, n. m., the river *Sicoris*, now Segre, a tributary of the Iberus near Ilerda.

flum-en, -inis, n. n., *river*.

pons, pontis, n. m., *bridge*.

efficio, efficere, effeci, effectum, v. a. 3, *make up, make, complete, construct*.

disto, v. n. defect. 1, *am distant, stand apart;* distantes inter se, *distant from one another*.

mille, indecl. in sing., pl. milia, milium, milibus, num. adj., *thousand;* mille passus or mille passuum, or simply mille, *a thousand paces, a* (Roman) *mile*, about 1618 yards, or 142 yards less than an English mile.

pass-us, -ūs, n. m., *pace*, about five (Roman, which are some-

what shorter than English) feet.

quattuor, num. adj., *four*.

nongent-i, -ae, -a, num. adj., *nine hundred*.

tripl-ex, -icis, adj., *threefold, in three lines*.

instruo, instruxi, instructum, v. a. 3, *draw up, marshal*.

aci-es, -ēi, n. f., *line of battle, battle-array, army*.

Ilerd-a, -ae, n. f., *Ilerda*, now Lerida, a city of Hispania Tarraconensis on the Sicoris.

coll-is, -is, n. m., *hill*.

ubi, adv., *where, when*.

tumūl-us, -i, n. m., *mound, hill*.

paulo, adv., *by a little, somewhat, a little*.

ēdit-us, -a, -um, part. adj., *high, lofty, elevated*.

commūnio, communivi and communii, communitum, v. a. 4, *fortify*.

commeāt-us, -ūs, n. m., *provisions, supplies*.

interclūdo, interclūsi, interclūsum, v. a. 3, with acc., and abl. with or without ab, *shut off, separate, cut off from*.

adversari-us, -a, -um, adj., *opposed to one;* adversari-us, -i, n. m., *antagonist, adversary, enemy*.

confido, confisus sum, v. n. 3, *trust, confide, am confident*.

13.

spēro, v. a. 1, *hope, hope for, expect*.

edūco, eduxi, eductum, v. a. 3, *lead out*.

antesignān-i (supply milites),
-orum, n. m., *soldiers who
fought before the standards,
men in the first line.*

procurro, procucurri and pro-
curri, procursum, v. n. 3,
run forward.

brev-is, -e, adj., *short.*

proeli-um, -i, n. n., *battle.*

prius, comp. adv., *before, sooner,
first.*

Afraniān-us, -a, -um, adj., *of or
belonging to Afranius;* Afraniani, n. m., *soldiers of
Afranius.*

nost-er, -ra, -rum, pronom. adj.,
our; nostri (supply milites),
our men, our troops.

repello, reppūli, repulsum, v.
a. 3, *drive back, repel.*

terg-um, -i, n. n., *back, rear:*
a tergo, *from behind, in rear;*
terga vertere, *to turn the
back, take to flight.*

verto, verti, versum, v. a. 3,
turn.

sign-um, -i, n. n., *standard,
sign, signal:* signa tollere,
to break up the camp.

recipio, recipĕre, recēpi, re-
ceptum, v. a. 3, *get back,
recover, receive, sustain;* se
recipere, *to retire, retreat,
fall back.*

cohortor, cohortātus sum, v.
dep. 1, *exhort.*

non-us, -a, -um, num. adj., *ninth.*

subsidi-um, -i, n. n., *support,
relief.*

duco, duxi, ductum, v. a. 3,
lead, draw out, prolong.

host-is, -is, com., *enemy.*

supprĭmo, suppressi, suppres-
sum, v. a. 3, *check.*

rursus, adv., *again.*

praefĕro, praeferre, praetŭli,
praelātum, v. a. irreg., *put
forward, express.*

opini-o, -ōnis, n. f., *opinion.*

uterque, utrăque, utrumque,
pron., *both, each, either.*

superi-or, -us, gen. -ōris, comp.
adj., *higher, superior, former.*

existĭmo, v. a. 1, *consider, think,
judge.*

pugno, v. n. 1, *fight.*

prim-us, -a, -um, superl. adj.,
first, foremost.

congress-us, -ūs, n. m., *meeting,
encounter.*

autem, conj., *but, on the other
hand, now, moreover.*

inīqu-us, -a, -um, adj., *uneven,
unfair, unfavourable.*

congredior, congrĕdi, congres-
sus sum, v. dep. 3, *come together, meet in battle.*

hor-a, -ae, n. f., *hour.*

sustĭneo, sustĭnui, sustentum,
v. a. 2, *hold up, sustain,
maintain, endure, withstand.*

compello, compŭli, compulsum,
v. a. 3, *drive, force.*

14.

intĕrim, adv., *meanwhile, in
the meantime.*

Oscens-es, -ium, n. m. pl., *the
inhabitants of Osca, now
Huesca in Aragon.*

Calagurritān-i, -orum, n. m.
pl., *the inhabitants of Calla-
gurris, now Loarre, north of
Osca.*

imperāt-um, -i, n. n., *order,*
command ; imperata facere,
to execute orders, obey.
făcio, făcĕre, fēci, factum, v.
a., *do, make.*
Tarraconens-es, -ium, n. m.
pl.,*the inhabitants of Tarraco,*
now Tarragona.
Iacetăn-i, -orum, n. m. pl., a
people in northern Spain, at
the foot of the Pyrenees, in
what is now called Catalonia.
Ausetan-i, -orum, n. m. pl., a
people of Hispania Tarra-
conensis, in what is now
Catalonia.
post, prep. gov. acc., *after,*
behind ; adv., *afterwards,*
after.
Ilurgavonens-es, -ium, n. m.
pl., a people of Hispania
Tarraconensis, on the sea
coast near the mouth of the
Ebro.
Hibĕr-us, -i, n. m., a river in
Spain, now the Ebro.
attingo, attīgi, attactum, v. a.
3, *touch, reach, border on,*
come to.
commutati-o,-ōnis,n. f.,*change.*
mult-us, -a, -um, adj., *much ;*
pl., *many ;* comp., plus,
pluris, in pl. plures, plura,
plurium ; superl., plurimus.
longinqu-us, -a, -um, adj.,
distant.
civit-as, -ātis, n. f., *state, com-*
munity.
descisco, descīvi or descii, de-
scitum, v. n., 3, *revolt.*
Celtiberi-a, -ae, n. f., *Celtiberia,*
the land of the Celtiberi, a

people of Middle Spain, who
originated by a mingling of
Celts with the original
Iberians.
bell-um, -i, n. n., *war.*
transfĕro, transferre, transtŭli,
translạtum, v. a. irreg.,
bring over, shift, transfer.
hic, adv., *here.*
equitāt-us, -us, n. m., *cavalry ;*
pl., *troops of horse.*
auxili-um, -i, n. n., *help, aid ;*
pl., *auxiliaries.*
hiems, hiĕmis, n. f.. *winter.*
cogĭto, v. a. 1, *think, plan, pur-*
pose.
ineo, inīre, inīvi or inii, initum,
v. a. and n., *enter, enter on,*
adopt.
conquīro, conquisīvi, conquisī-
tum, v. a. 3, *search for, hunt*
up.
Octogēs-a, -ae, n. f., a town of
Hispania Tarraconensis, at
the spot where the Sicoris
flows into the Hiberus, the
modern Mequinenza, near La
Granja.
addūco, adduxi, adductum, v.
a. 3, *bring to, induce, prompt.*
trigintā, num. adj. indecl.,
thirty.
iungo, iunxi, iunctum, v. a. 3,
join, fasten together.
tradūco, traduxi, traductum,
v. a. 3, *lead across,bring over.*

15.

aliqui, aliqua, aliquod, indef.
pronom. adj., *some.*
vad-um, -i, n. n., *ford, shoal,*
shallow water.

E

huc, adv., *hither, to this point.*
redūco, reduxi, reductum, v. a. 3, *lead back, bring* (to a state).
audeo, ausus sum, v. a. and n. 2, *dare.*
ped-es, ĭtĭs, n. m., *foot-soldier;* pl., *infantry.*
altĭtūd-o, -ĭnis, n. f., *depth.*
aqua, aquae, n. f., *water.*
tum, adv., *then;* cum ... tum, *both ... and.*
rapidĭt-as, -ātis, n. f., *swift-ness, speed.*
relinquo, relīqui, relictum, v. a. 3, *leave.*
nĭsi, conj., *if not, unless.*
agmen, agmĭnis, n. n., *army on the march, train, march.*
mălĕ, adv., *badly;* male habere, *annoy, hamper.*
carpo, carpsi, carptum, v. a. 3, *harass.*
vĭgĭli-a, ae, n. f., *watch* (of the night).
nov-us, -a, -um, adj., *new;* superl., novissimus, *last, hindmost;* novissimum ag-men, *rear-guard.*
incĭpĭo, incĭpĕre, incēpi, incep-tum, v. a. and n., *begin.*

16.

lux, lūcis, n. f., *light.*
cert-us, -a, -um, adj., *certain, fixed;* certiorem (aliquem) facere, *to inform, tell.*
eā (supply via or parte), adv., *by that way, there.*
quā, adv., *where.*
magnĭtūd-o, -ĭnis, n. f., *great-ness, large volume.*

obĭcio, obĭcĕre, obieci, obiectum, v. a. 3, *expose, put in way of.*
conor, conātus sum, v. dep. 1, *make an attempt, attempt.*
experior, expertus sum, v. dep. 4, *try, make trial of.*
iudĭco, v. a. 1, *judge, consider.*
centurĭ-a, -ae, n. f., *century, company,* theoretically con-sisting of one hundred men, but, for the most part, really little over half that number.
delĭgo, delēgi, delectum, v. a. 3, *pick out, choose.*
aut, conj., *or;* aut ... aut, *either ... or.*
vis, acc. vim, abl. vi, n. f., *force, violence, quantity, number;* pl., vires, virium, *strength, power.*
expedĭt-us, -a, -um, part. adj., *lightly equipped, in light marching order, unimpeded, free, easy.*
iument-um, -i, n. n., *beast of burden.*
suprā, adv., *above.*
infrā, adv., *below.*

17.

conspĭcio, conspĭcĕre, conspexi, conspectum, v. a. 3, *catch sight of, descry.*
camp-us, -i, n. m., *plain.*
reficio, reficĕre, refēci, refectum, v. a. 3, *repair, refresh, re-cruit, rest.*
defess-us, -a, -um, part. (of defetiscor), *tired, exhausted.*
progrĕdior, progrĕdi, progressus sum, v. dep. 3, *go forth, advance.*

necessario, adv., *of necessity,
unavoidably.*
matūrē, adv., *soon, early;*
comp. maturius; superl.,
maturissīmē and maturrīmē.
quam, adv., *than.*
quŏque, conj., *also, too.*
medi-us, -a, -um, adj., *middle;*
media nox, *midnight.*
circīter, adv., *about.*
dux, dūcis, n. m., *leader,
general.*
vas, vasis, pl. vasa, vasorum,
n. n., *utensil, implement;*
as a military term, *baggage.*
militar-is, -e, adj., *of or belonging to a soldier, military.*
mos, mōris, n. m., *custom,
usage, manner.*
exaudio, exaudīvi or exaudii,
exaudītum, v. a. 4, *hear,
overhear.*
clam-or, ōris, n. m., *shout, cry,
shouting.*
vereor, verītus sum, v. dep. a.
and n. 2, *fear.*
noctu, adv., *by night.*
impedīt-us, -a, -um, pass. part.
(of impedio, 9), *embarrassed,
encumbered.*
onus, onĕris, n. n., *burden,
load.*
conflīgo, conflixi, conflictum,
v. n. 3, *engage, fight.*
contĭneo, continui, contentum,
v. a. 2, *hold together, keep together, confine, detain.*
occultē, adv., *secretly.*
explōro, v. a. 1, *examine, view,
reconnoitre.*
Decidi-us, -i, n. m., *a proper
name.*

Sax-a, -ae, n. m., *a surname of*
L. Decidius, *a partisan of*
Caesar.
natūr-a, -ae, n. f., *nature,
character.*
perspicio, perspicĕre, perspexi,
perspectum, v. a. 3, *examine,
look into.*
renuntio, v. a. 1, *bring back
word, report.*
intercēdo, intercessi, inter-
cessum, v. n. 3, *intervene,
come between, exist between.*
campest-er, -ris, -re, adj., *of or
belonging to a plain, level, flat.*
inde, adv., *thence, after that.*
excĭpio, excĭpĕre, excēpi, ex-
ceptum, v. a. 3, *catch, catch
up, follow after, succeed, receive, await.*
asp-er, -ĕra, -ĕrum, adj., *rough,
rugged.*
montŭōs-us,-a,-um, adj., *mountainous.*
pri-or, -us, gen. -ōris, comp.
adj., *former, first* (of two).
angusti-ae, -arum, n. f. pl.,
*narrow pass, defile, difficul-
ties.*
prohĭbeo, prohibui, prohibĭtum,
v. a. 2, *keep in check, hinder,
forbid.*

18.

circŭīt-us, -ūs, n. m., *circuit,
round, detour, way round,
compass.*
null-us, -a, -um, adj., *no, none,
not any.*
nam, adv., *for.*
pertĭneo, pertinui, v. n. 2,
stretch out, extend to.

oppōno, oppŏsui, oppŏsĭtum, v. a. 3, *set against, oppose.*

ac. conj. *and.*

primo, adv., *at first.*

viso, visi, visum, v. a. 3, *view, visit, see.*

laet-us, -a, -um, adj., *glad, joyful.*

contumeliŏs-us, -a, -um, adj., *insulting.*

prosĕquor, prosĕqui, prosecūtus sum, v. dep., *escort, attend, pursue:* vocibus prosequi, *to shout after.*

proposĭt-um, -i, n. n., *purpose, intention, plan, design.*

divers-us, -a, -um, part. (of diverto), *turned a different way, in a different direction, different, opposite.*

contrari-us, -a, -um, adj., *contrary, opposite.*

ĕo, ire, ivi or ii, ĭtum, v. n. 4, *go.*

paulātim, adv., *little by little, gradually.*

retorqueo, retorsi, retortum, v. a. 2, *bend back, turn back.*

dextr-a, -ae, n. f., *right-hand.*

supĕro, v. a. and n. 1, *go past, pass beyond, overcome, conquer.*

adverto, adverti, adversum, v. a. 3, *turn to;* animum advertere, also as one word animadvertere, *to turn the mind to, to observe, notice.*

exeo, exire, exĭvi or exii, exĭtum, v. n. 4, *go out, march out.*

rect-us, -a, -um, part. adj., *straight.*

celerĭt-as, -ātis, n. f., *speed, swiftness.*

certām-en, -ĭnis, n. n., *contest.*

uter, utra, utrum, gen. utrius, pron., *which of two.*

mons, montis, n. m., *mountain, hill.*

rup-es, -is, n. f., *rock, cliff.*

nanciscor, nancisci, nactus sum, v. dep. 3, *obtain, gain, reach, meet with.*

planiti-es, -ei, n. f., *plain.*

contrā, prep. gov. acc., *against.*

ante, prep. gov. acc. and adv., *before.*

quidam, quaedam, quoddam, pron., *a certain, somebody.*

19.

occasi-o, -ōnis, n. f., *opportunity.*

bĕnĕ, adv., *well.*

sĭnĕ, prep. gov. abl., *without.*

pugn-a, -ae, n. f., *fight, battle,*

vuln-us, -ĕris, n. n., *wound, loss.*

premo, pressi, pressum, v. a. 3, *press hard, distress.*

pabulati-o, -ōnis, n. f., *foraging.*

aquor, v. dep. 1, *fetch water.*

cotidie, adv., *daily.*

perfŭgio, perfŭgĕre, perfūgi, v. n. 3, *desert.*

explicĭt-us, -a, -um, part. adj., *free from difficulties, easy.*

revertor, reverti, reversus sum, v. dep. 3, *return.*

paul-um, -i, n. n., *a little.*

frument-um, -i, n. n., *corn, grain.*

Tarrac-o, -ōnis, n. f., a town in Spain, now Tarragona.

longē, adv., *far off*; comp., **longius** ; superl., longissĭmē.

spati-um, -i, n. n., *space, distance, interval, period*.

cas-us, -ūs, n. m., *fall, disaster, misfortune, accident, event ;* **casu**, *by chance, as it chanced.*

intellĕgo,intellexi,intellectum, v. a. 3, *understand, perceive.*

acrĭter, adv., *fiercely, eagerly, with spirit.*

complūr-es, -a and -ia, gen. -ium, adj. or subst., *several, very many.*

interfĭcio, interfĭcĕre, interfēci, interfectum, v. a. 3, *kill.*

procul, adv., *far off, at a distance.*

tandem, adv., *at length, at last.*

obsĭdeo, obsēdi, obsessum, v. a. 2, *beset, besiege, hamper.*

lign-um, -i, n. n., *wood ;* pl., *firewood.*

inopi-a, -ae, n. f., *want, scarcity.*

colloqui-um, -i, n. n., *conference, parley.*

audio, audīvi or audii, audītum, v. a. 4, *hear.*

perpetior, perpĕti, perpessus sum, v. dep. 3, *endure to the end, bear steadfastly, suffer.*

nunc, adv., *now.*

neque or **nec**, conj., *and not, nor ;* **neque ... neque**, *neither ... nor.*

corp-us, -ŏris, n. n., *body.*

dol-or, -ōris, n. m., *pain.*

ignomini-a, -ae, n. f., *disgrace, ignominy.*

fero, ferre, tŭli, lātum, v. a. irreg., *bear, carry, suffer, resist, propose* (a law).

vinco, vīci, victum, v. a. 3, *conquer.*

confĭteor, confessus sum, v. dep. 2, *confess.*

respondeo,respondi,responsum, v. a. 2, *answer, reply.*

nemo, nemĭnis (but in classical Latin nullīus, from nullus, is used as the gen. and nullō, nullā as the abl.), pron., *no one.*

noceo, nocui, nocitum, v. n. 2, with dat., *harm, do hurt to.*

provinci-a, -ae, n. f., *province.*

20.

diffīdo, diffīsus sum, v. n. 3, with dat., *distrust.*

Pompeiān-us, -a, -um, adj., *of or belonging to Pompey :* **Pompeian**-i, -orum, n. m., *the soldiers of Pompey, Pompey's party :* **Pompeianae res**, *Pompey's cause* or *side.*

amĭcē, adv., *in a friendly manner ;* superl., amicissĭmē.

ull-us,-a,-um,adj.,*any,any one.*

posteā, adv., *afterwards.*

Massĭli-a, -ae, n. f., *a seaport town in Gallia Narbonensis,* now Marseilles.

detĭneo, detinui, detentum, v. a. 2, *keep back, detain.*

coniungo,coniunxi,coniunctum, v. a. 3, *join, unite.*

convĕnio, convēni, conventum, v. n. and a. 4, *come together, assemble, muster, meet with.*

lātē, adv., *broadly, widely, in an exaggerated manner ;* comp., **latius** ; superl., latissĭmē.

inflāte, adv., *haughtily,proudly, pompously;* comp., **inflatius**.

perscrībo, perscripsi, perscriptum, v. a. 3, *write in full* or *at length, detail.*

mot-us, -ūs, n. m., *motion, movement, change.*

fortūn-a, -ae, n. f., *fortune, luck.*

coepi, coepisse, v. a. and n., *defect.* (properly the perf. of coepio, the imperfect tenses of which are not used by classical writers), *begin.*

paro, v. a. 1, *prepare.*

Gād-es, -ium, n. f., now Cadiz, a colony of the Phoenicians in Hispania Baetica, on an island close to the shore.

longius, see longe, **28**.

consentio, consensi, consensum, v. n. 4, *agree, determine in common.*

Gaditān-i, -ōrum, n. m., *the inhabitants of Gades.*

princeps, princĭpis, n. and adj., *first, chief, chief man.*

insŭl-a, -ae, n. f., *island.*

servo, v. a. 1, *preserve, keep.*

21.

adsto, adstiti, v. n., *stand near, stand by.*

inspecto, v. a. 1 (classical only in pres. part.), *look on, look at, observe.*

Hispāl-is, -is, n. f., a city of Hispania Baetica, now Seville.

perterreo, perterrui, perterrĭtum, v. a. 2, *frighten* or *terrify thoroughly.*

converto, converti, conversum, v. a. and n. 3, *turn round, wheel about, change.*

Italĭc-a, -ae, n. f., a city in Hispania Baetica, near Seville, now Santiponce.

praeclūdo, praeclūsi, praeclūsum, v. a. 3, *shut to, close, shut against* one.

Sext-us, -i, n. m., a Roman praenomen.

praesto, adv., *at hand, ready, present;* **praesto esse**, *to be at hand, attend* or *wait upon, aid.*

conti-o, -ōnis, n. f., *assembly, speech;* **contionem habere**, *to deliver a speech.*

bidu-um, -i, n. n., *space of two days.*

Cordŭb-a, -ae, n. f., a town in Hispania Baetica, on the river Baetis, now Cordova.

commŏror, v. dep. 1, *tarry, remain.*

Q., abbrev. for **Quintus**, a Roman praenomen or forename.

Cassi-us, -i, n. m., a Roman gentile name.

praefĭcio, praefĭcĕre, praefēci, praefectum, v. a. 3, with acc. and dat., *set over,appoint to the command of.*

Narb-o, -ōnis, n. m., a city in Gaul, from which Gallia Narbonensis takes its name, now Narbonne.

lex, lēgis, n. f., *law.*

dictāt-or, -ōris, n. m., *dictator,* a chief magistrate appointed by the Romans for six months in seasons of emergency, and armed with absolute authority.

Lepĭd-us, -i, n. m., a Roman surname.

22.

dum, conj., *while, whilst.*

Trebonĭ-us, -i, n. m., a Roman gentile name. **C. Trebonius** was a legate of Caesar in Gaul.

oppugnati-o, -ōnis, n. f., *siege.*

agger, aggĕris, n. m., *mound.*

vine-a, -ae, n. f., *penthouse, shed, mantlet*, built like an arbor for sheltering besiegers.

turr-is, -is, n. f., *tower.*

antiquĭtus, adv., *from ancient times, of old.*

apparāt-us, -ūs, n. m., *preparation, provision, equipment.*

multitūd-o, -ĭnis, n. f., *multitude, number.*

torment-um, -i, n. n., *engine for hurling missiles.*

contexo, contexui, contextum, v. a. 3, *entwine, interweave.*

vim-en, -ĭnis, n. n., *a pliant twig, withe, osier.*

Massiliens-es, -ium, n. m., *inhabitants of Massilia.*

mal-um, -i, n. n., *evil, misfortune, suffering.*

bis, adverbial num., *twice.*

navāl-is, -e, *of* or *belonging to ships, naval.*

creb-er,-ra,-rum, adj.,*frequent, numerous, repeated.*

erupti-o, -ōnis, n. f., *sally.*

fundo, fudi, fusum, v. a. 3, *overthrow, rout.*

grav-is, -e, adj., *heavy, severe, grievous.*

pestilenti-a,-ae, n. f., *pestilence, plague.*

conflicto, v. a. 1, *afflict, ruin, overwhelm.*

dēdo, dēdĭdi, dēdĭtum, v. a. 3, *give up; se dedere, to surrender, capitulate.*

compăro, v. a. 1, *prepare, provide, make ready.*

turbĭd-us, -a, -um, adj., *wild, stormy.*

tempest-as, -ātis, n. f., *weather.*

conspect-us, -ūs, n. m., *range* or *reach of sight, view.*

abeo, abīre, abĭvi or abii, abĭtum, v. n. 4, *go away, depart.*

profĕro, proferre, protŭli, prolatum, v. a. irreg., *bring forth.*

publĭc-um, -i, n. n., *public purse, public treasury.*

23.

Curi-o, -ōnis, n. m., a surname in the gens Scribonia.

Afrĭc-a, -ae, n. f., *Africa.*

Sicĭli-a, -ae, n. f., *Sicily.*

appello, appŭli, appulsum, v. a. and n. 3, *put in to shore, land.*

appello, v. a. 1, *call by name, address, entitle, name.*

Anquillari-a, -ae, n. f., a town on the Gulf of Carthage, to the south of the Promunturium Mercurii or Cape Bon.

Utíc-a, -ae, n. f., a town in Africa, north of Carthage, now Boushater.

vall-um, -i, n. n., *stockade, rampart.*

circummunio, circummunivi, circummunitum, v. a. 4, *wall up around, fortify, secure.*

insolens, insolentis, adj., with gen., *unaccustomed to.*

diuturnít-as, -ātis, n. f., *long duration.*

oti-um, -i, n. n., *inactivity, ease, repose, peace.*

dediti-o, -ōnis, n. f., *surrender, capitulation.*

palam, adv., *openly, publicly.*

nunti-us, -i, n. m., *messenger.*

rex, rēgis, n. m., *king.*

Iub-a, -ae, n. m., a Numidian king, who joined the party of Pompey, gained a victory over Caesar's legate Curio, and put an end to his own life after the battle of Thapsus.

custodi-a, -ae, n. f., *guard, care, protection.*

defensi-o, -ōnis, n. f., *defending, defence.*

hortor, v. dep. 1, *encourage, cheer, exhort.*

simult-as, -ātis, n. f., *dissension, enmity, jealousy.*

promulgo, v. a. 1, *promulgate, publish, propose.*

regn-um, -i, n. n., *kingdom.*

publico, v. a. 1, *confiscate.*

perfüg-a, -ae, n. m., *deserter.*

revŏco, v. a. 1, *recall.*

finitím-us, -a, -um, adj., *bordering upon, adjoining, neighbouring.*

resisto, restiti, v. n. 3, *halt, stop, stay behind, remain, withstand, resist.*

Saburr-a, -ae, n. m., a lieutenant of King Juba.

praefect-us, -i, n. m., *chief, commander, prefect.*

mediocr-is, -e, adj., *moderate.*

appropinquo, v. n. 1, *draw near, approach.*

auct-or, -ōris, n. m., *one by whose influence or advice anything is done, instigator, counsellor, adviser.*

temĕrē, adv., *heedlessly, thoughtlessly, rashly.*

credo, credidi, creditum, v. a. 3, with dat., *give as a loan, entrust, trust to, confide in, believe;* **credita pecunia,** *a loan.*

committo, commisi, commissum, v. a. 3, *entrust, commit.*

Bagrăd-a, -ae, n. m., a river in Africa, near Utica, now Medscherda.

praesum, praeesse, praefui, v. n. irreg., with dat., *am set over, have command of.*

nocte, adv., *by night.*

imprūdens, imprudentis, adj., *not anticipating, unaware, off one's guard.*

inopinans, inopinantis, adj., *not expecting, unprepared.*

Numíd-a, -ae, n. m., *a Numidian;* the Numidians were a people of northern Africa, between Mauretania and the territory of Carthage, in the modern Algiers.

aggredior, aggredi, aggressus sum, v. dep. 3, *attack, undertake, begin.*

24.

quart-us, -a, -um, num. adj., *fourth.*

sex, num. adj. indecl., *six.*

accelero, v. a. 1, *hasten, accelerate.*

at, conj., *but.*

ali-us, -a, -ud, adj. and subst., *another, other* (of many); **alii alio loco,** *some in one place and some in another.*

nocturn-us, -a, -um, adj., *of or belonging to night, nocturnal, by night, in the night.*

submitto, submisi, submissum, v. a. 3, *send secretly, despatch.*

elephant-us, -i, n. m., *elephant.*

sexaginta, num. adj., *sixty.*

lente, adv., *slowly, leisurely;* comp., **lentius.**

simulati-o, -onis, n. f., *pretence.*

cedo, cessi, cessum, v. n. 3, *go, withdraw, retire, retreat.*

pes, pedis, n. m., *foot.*

fugio, fugere, fugi, fugitum, v. n. 3, *flee, fly, take to flight.*

arbitror, v. dep. 1, *am of opinion, believe, think.*

circumeo, circumire, circumivi or circumii, circuitum, v. n. and a. 4, *go round, surround, encompass.*

quidem, adv., *indeed;* **ne ... quidem,** *not even.*

lab-or, -oris, n. m., *toil, labour, exertion.*

studi-um, -i, n. n., *zeal, eagerness.*

virt-us, -utis, n. f., *courage.*

ducent-i, -ae, -a, num. adj., *two hundred.*

25.

crebro, adv., *repeatedly, often.*

augeo, auxi, auctum, v. a. 2, *increase, reinforce.*

lassitud-o, -inis, n. f., *weariness, fatigue.*

deficio, deficere, defeci, defectum, v. a. and n., *fail.*

simul, adv., *at the same time.*

circumdo, circumdare, circumdedi, circumdatum, v. a., *enclose, surround.*

numquam, adv., *never.*

amitto, amisi, amissum, v. a. 3, *lose.*

ita, adv., *thus, so.*

proelior, v. dep. 1, *engage in battle, fight.*

perpauc-i, -ae, -a, adj., *very few.*

Marci-us, -i, n. m., Roman gentile name.

quaest-or, -oris, n. m., *quaestor,* a Roman magistrate or officer.

obsecro, v. a. 1, *entreat, beg.*

reporto, v. a. 1, *carry back.*

lenuncul-us, -i, n. m., *bark, skiff.*

imperi-um, -i, n. n., *command, order, authority.*

lit-us, -oris, n. n., *shore.*

contenti-o, -onis, n. f., *struggle, contest.*

potissimum, adv., *chiefly, in preference to all others, first.*

nonnull-i, -ae, -a, adj., *several, some.*

deprĭmo, depressi, depressum, v. a. 3, *press down, sink.*

prope, prep. with acc., *near;* adv., *almost;* comp., propĭus.

adeo, adire, adii, aditum, v. n. and a., *approach, go to.*

tardo, v. a. 1, *delay, hinder, prevent.*

accĭdo, accĭdi, v. n. 3, *fall out, happen, occur.*

Var-us, -i, n. m., a Roman surname.

conspĭcor, conspicātus sum, v. dep. 1, *get sight of, see, perceive.*

praedĭco, v. a. 1, *proclaim, declare, say.*

praed-a, -ae, n. f., *booty, spoil.*

elect-us, -a, -um, part. adj., *picked, selected.*

remitto, remīsi, remissum, v. a. 3, *send back.*

26.

comĭti-um, -i, n. n., the place for the assembling of the Romans voting by the curiae; pl., the assembly of the Romans for electing magistrates, etc., the *comitia;* comitia habere, *to hold the elections.*

creo, v. a. 1, *create, choose, elect.*

Iuli-us, -i, n. m., a Roman gentile name.

P., abbrev. for Publius, a Roman forename.

Servili-us, -i, n. m., a Roman gentile name.

fid-es, -ei, n. f., *faith, credit* (as a commercial term).

angust-us,-a,-um,adj., *narrow, contracted, weakened.*

arbĭt-er, -ri, n. m., *arbiter, umpire, judge.*

aestimati-o, -ōnis, n. f., *valuation, appraisement.*

possessi-o, -ōnis, n. f., *possession, property, estate.*

quant-us, -a, -um, adj., *how great;* quanti, gen. of price, *how dear, at what price, of what value.*

credĭt-or, -ōris, n. m., *creditor.*

tabŭl-a, -ae, n. f., *a writing-tablet;* pl., *a book of account:* novae tabulae, *new account-books,* by substituting which for the old ones debts were abolished, *cancelling* or *abolition of debts.*

minuo, minui, minūtum, v. a. 3, *lessen, diminish, abate.*

ferē, adv., *nearly, almost, for the most part.*

civĭl-is, -e, adj., *of* or *pertaining to citizens, civil, civic.*

dissensi-o, -ōnis, n. f. *disagreement, dissension, discord.*

consuesco,consuēvi,consuētum, v. n. 3., *am accustomed, am wont.*

debĭt-or, -ōris, n. m., *debtor.*

existimati-o, -ōnis, n. f., *reputation, credit.*

apt-us, -a, -um, part. adj., *suited, adapted, fit.*

item, adv., *likewise, in like manner.*

ambĭt-us, -ūs, n. m., *canvassing, corruption, bribery.*

damno, v. a. 1, *condemn, sentence.*

VOCABULARY. 55

intĕg-er, -ra, -rum, adj., *whole, entire, unimpaired, unexhausted, unrounded;* in integrum restituere, *to restore to a former condition or state.*
restituo, restitui, restitūtum, v. a. 3, *put back again, replace, restore.*
feri-ae, -arum, n. f. pl., *holidays, festival.*
Latīn-us, -a, -um, adj., *of* or *belonging to Latium, Latin;* feriae Latinae, *the festival of the allied Latins,* which was celebrated especially by offerings to Juppiter Latiaris on Mons Albanus.
perfĭcio, perfícére, perfēci, perfectum, v. a. 3, *complete, accomplish.*
undĕcim, num. adj. indecl., *eleven.*
tribuo, tribui, tribūtum, v. a. 3, *assign, allot, give.*
dictatūr-a, -ae, n. f., *office of dictator, dictatorship.*
abdĭco, v. a. 1, *disown, renounce;* se abdicare, with abl., *to resign* an office.

27.

duodĕcim, num. adj., *twelve.*
angustē, adv., *within narrow limits, hardly.*
quindĕcim, num. adj., *fifteen.*
legionari-us, -a, -um, adj., *of* or *belonging to a legion, legionary.*
sexcent-i, -ae, -a, num. adj., *six hundred.*
transporto, v. a. 1, *carry across, transport.*

annu-us, -a, -um, adj., *of a year's duration.*
vacu-us, -a, -um, adj., *empty, free from.*
otiōs-us, -a, -um, adj., *tranquil, undisturbed.*
class-is, -is, n. f., *fleet.*
civ-is, -is, n. com., *citizen.*
novem, num. adj., *nine.*
hiĕmo, v. n. 1, *pass the winter, keep in winter-quarters.*
Apolloni-a, -ae, n. f., a town in Illyria.
maritĭm-us, -a, -um, adj., *on the sea-coast, sea-.*
or-a, -ae, n. f., *coast.*
quicumque, quaecumque, quodcumque, rel. pron., *whoever, whatever.*
aequ-us, -a, -um, adj., *even, equal, fair;* aequo animo, *with equanimity, patiently.*
postridiē, adv., *the following day, next day.*
terr-a, -ae, n. f., *land, earth.*
Cerauni-i, -ōrum (also Cerauni-a, -orum), n. m., a ridge of mountains in Epirus on the borders of Illyria, *Ceraunian promontory, Acrocraunia.*
sax-um, -i, n. n., *rock.*
periculōs-us, -a, -um, adj., *dangerous.*
quiĕt-us, -a, -um, adj., *quiet, calm.*
stati-o, -ōnis, n. f., *anchorage, roadstead.*
Palaest-ē, -ēs, n. f., a seaport in Epirus.
expōno, expōsui, expōsĭtum, v. a. 3, *set out, disembark.*

28.

sērō, adv., *late, too late;* comp., serius.

provĕho, provexi, provectum, v. a. 3, *carry forwards;* pass., *go, proceed, set sail.*

ūtor, ūti, ūsus sum, v. dep. 3, *use, enjoy, take advantage of.*

aur-a, -ae, n. f., *breeze.*

offendo, offendi, offensum, v. a. and n. 3, *strike against, suffer damage.*

Bibŭl-us, -i, n. m., a proper name.

Corcȳr-a, -ae, n. f., an island in the Ionian Sea, now Corfu.

inān-is, -e, adj., *empty.*

occurro, occurri, occursum, v. n. 3, *run to meet, meet, fall in with.*

incendo, incendi, incensum, v. a. 3, *set fire to, set on fire.*

ign-is, -is, n. m., *fire.*

naut-a, -ae, n. m., *sailor.*

domĭn-us, -i, n. m., *master, owner.*

longē, adv., *far, far off;* longe lateque, *far and wide;* comp., longius.

29.

Octavi-us, -i, n. m., a Roman gentile name.

Salōn-ae, -arum, n. f., a maritime town in Dalmatia. Its ruins, still called Salona, lie near Spalato.

oppugno, v. a. 1, *attack, assault, besiege.*

munio, munīvi or munii, munitum, v. a. 4, *fortify, defend.*

propter, prep. gov. acc., *on account of.*

paucit-as, -ātis, n. f., *fewness.*

hom-o, -ĭnis, n. m., *man.*

descendo, descendi, descensum, v. n. 3, *descend, have recourse to.*

serv-us, -i, n. m., *slave.*

pubes or puber, pubĕris, adj., *of ripe age, adult.*

libĕro, v. a. 1, *set free.*

quin-i, -ae, -a, distrib. num. adj., *five each, five.*

meridiān-us, -a, -um, adj., *of or belonging to mid-day, mid-day.*

irrumpo, irrūpi, irruptum, v. n. 3, *burst in.*

confūgio, confūgĕre, confūgi, v. n. 3, *flee for refuge.*

despēro, v. a. and n. 1, *despair, despair of, give up.*

30.

benefici-um, -i, n. n., *favour, benefit.*

idone-us, -a, -um, adj., *fit, suitable.*

mandāt-um, -i, n. n., *charge, commission, command.*

auctorit-as, -ātis, n. f., *authority, influence.*

Candavi-a, -ae, n. f., a mountainous district in Illyria.

Macedoni-a, -ae, n. f., *Macedonia, Macedon,* a country between Thessaly and Thrace.

perturbo, v. a. 1, *disturb, trouble, embarrass.*

Oric-um, -i, n. n., a sea-port town of Illyria, now Ericho.

quo, adv., *whither;* with comp., *in order that, so that.*

Torquāt-us, n. m., *a Roman surname.*

iuss-us, -ūs, n. m., *order, command.*

interpōno, interpŏsui, interpositum, v. n. 3, *interpose, introduce.*

Apolloniāt-es, -ium, n. m. pl., *the inhabitants of Apollonia.*

31.

diurn-us, -a, -um, adj., *by day, in the day.*

mētor, mētātus sum, v. dep. 1, *measure off, mark, lay out.*

praeoccŭpo, v. a. 1, *seize upon, occupy beforehand, preoccupy.*

fin-is, -is, n. m., *end;* pl., *bor ders, territory.*

propĕro, v. n. 1, *hasten.*

Aps-us, -i, n. m., *a river of Illyria.*

pell-is, -is, n. f., *skin, hide, tent;* sub pellibus hiemare, *to winter under canvas, in camp.*

trans, prep. gov. acc., *across, beyond.*

condūco, conduxi, conductum, v.a.3, *draw together, assemble, collect.*

32.

mens-is, -is, n. m., *month.*

praecipĭto, v. n. 1, *come to an end, close.*

praetermitto, praetermĭsi, praetermissum, v. a. 3, *let pass, omit, neglect.*

severē, adv., *severely, harshly;* comp., severius.

scribo, scripsi, scriptum, v. a. 3, *write.*

vent-us, -i, n. m., *wind.*

navĭgo, v. n. 1, *sail.*

administro, v. a. 1, *manage, guide.*

Fufi-us, -i, n. m., *a Roman gentile name.*

Calēn-us, -i, n. m., *a proper name.*

aust-er, -ri, n. m., *south wind.*

praetervĕhor, praetervectus sum, v. dep. 3, *sail past.*

Nymphae-um, -i, n. n., *a promontory and seaport in Illyria, now Capo di Redeni.*

introdūco, introduxi, introductum, v. a. 3, *conduct into, bring in.*

amb-o, -ae, -o, adj., *both.*

insidi-ae, -arum, n. f. plur., *ambush, ambuscade.*

adorior, adortus sum, v. dep., 4, *assault, attack.*

statīv-us, -a, -um, adj., *standing still, stationary;* castra stativa, *a stationary camp,* a camp where an army halts for a long time.

clam, adv., *secretly.*

interdiu, adv., *by day.*

collŏco, v.a.1, *place, station, post.*

occult-us, -a, -um, adj., *hidden, concealed, secret.*

Graec-us, -i, n. m., *a Greek.*

defĕro, deferre, detŭli, delātum, v. a. irreg., *report, announce.*

circumclūdo, circumclusi, circumclusum, v. a. 3, *shut in, hem in.*

Asparagi-um, -i, n. n., a town
of Illyria on the river Genu-
sus, now Iskarpar.

33.

postquam,adv.,*after that,when.*
ĕŏdem, adv., *to the same place.*
difficil-is, -e, adj., *difficult.*
explorāt-or, -ōris, n. m., *scout,
spy.*
sūspĭcor, v. dep. 1, *suspect,
surmise, apprehend.*
adhortor, v. dep. 1, *exhort,
encourage, incite.*
parv-us, -a, -um, adj., *small,
little.*
intermitto, intermīsi, intermis-
sum, v. a. 3, *discontinue,
break off, interrupt, suffer to
elapse.*
māne, adv., *in the morning.*
cerno, crēvi, crētum, v. a. 3,
perceive, discern, see.
Petr-a, -ae, n. f., a hill near
Dyrrhachium.
adĭt-us, -ūs, n. m., *approach,
access.*
protĕgo, protexi, protectum, v.
a. 3, *protect, shelter.*

34.

depello, depŭli, depulsum, v.
a. 3, *drive away, deter, divert.*
commūto, v. a. 1, *change.*
impediment-um, -i, n. n., *hin-
derance ;* pl., *baggage.*
infĕro, inferre, intŭli, illātum,
v. a. irreg., *introduce, occa-
sion, cause.*
sauci-us,-a, -um, adj., *wounded,
sick.*

depōno, deposui, deposĭtum, v.
a. 3, *put aside, get rid of,
dispose of, give up.*
necesse, n. adj., *necessary.*
incĭto, v. a. 1, *incite, spur
on.*
si, conj., *if.*
illo, adv., *thither, to that place.*
nolo, nolle, nolui, v. n. irreg.,
am unwilling.
direct-us, -a, -um, part. adj.,
straight, direct.
accēdo, accessi, accessum, v.
n. 3, *approach, am added.*
improvīs-us, -a, -um, adj., *un-
foreseen ;* ex improviso, *unexpectedly.*
incommŏd-um, -i, n. n., *incon-
venience, trouble.*
Heracli-a, -ae, n. f., a town of
Macedonia, now Bitolia.
sublcio, subiēci, subiectum, v.
n. 3, *lay under, place near,
expose to.*
Allobrŏg-es,-um, n. m., a people
of Gallia Narbonensis.
profecti-o, -ōnis, n. f., *setting
out, departure.*
vix, adv., *hardly, barely.*
antecēdo, antecessi, anteces-
sum, v. n. 3, *go before, get
the start.*
vito, v. a. 1, *avoid, evade.*
Aegini-um, -i, n. n., a fortress
in Thessaly, now Kalabaka
or Stagous.
Thessali-a, -ae, n. f., *Thessaly.*

35.

Gomph-i, -orum, n. m., a town of
Thessaly, not far from Trik-
kala.

Epīr-us, -i, n. f., a province in
the north of Greece.
alt-us, -a, -um, part. adj., *high.*
moeni-a, -um, n. n. pl., *walls,*
ramparts.
sol, solis, n. m., *sun.*
occās-us, -ūs, n. m., *going down,*
setting.
expugno, v. a. 1, *take by assault,*
storm, capture.
dirĭpio, dirĭpěre, diripui, di-
reptum, v. a. 3, *plunder.*
concēdo, concessi, concessum,
v. a. 3, *grant, yield, give*
over.
Metropŏl-is, -is, n. f., a town
of Thessaly, between Gomphi
and Pharsalus.
Metropolīt-ae, -arum and -um,
n. m., inhabitants of Metropolis.
Gomphens-is, -e, adj., *of* or
belonging to Gomphi; Gom-
phens-es, -ium, n. m., the
inhabitants of Gomphi.
diligenter, adv., *carefully;*
comp., diligentius; superl.,
diligentissime.
conservo, v. a. 1, *preserve, save,*
leave unharmed.
praeter, prep. gov. acc., *besides,*
except.
Larisae-i, -ōrum, n. m., *inhabit-*
ants of Larissa, Larissaeans.
quin, conj., *that not, but that,*
but.
pareo, parui, parītum, v. n. 2,
with dat., *obey, submit to.*
plen-us, -a, -um, adj., with
gen., *full of, filled with,*
abounding in.
matūr-us, -a, -um, adj., *ripe.*

36.

cunct-us, -a, -um, adj., *all in a*
body, the whole, all.
hon-or, -ōris, n. m., *honour,*
dignity.
pristĭn-us, -a, -um, adj., *former,*
early, original.
victori-a, -ae, n. f., *victory.*
adeo, adv., *so, so much.*
quando, adv., *at any time, ever,*
chiefly after si, num, or ne.
tardē, adv., *slowly;* comp.,
tardius; superl., tardissĭmē.
considerātē, adv., *deliberately;*
comp.,consideratius; superl.,
consideratissĭmē.
delecto, v. a. 1, *delight, please,*
charm.
consulār-is, -is, n. m., *one who*
has been consul, an ex-consul.
praetori-us, -i, n. m., *one who*
has been praetor, an ex-
praetor.
postrēmo, adv., *finally, at last.*
praemi-um, -i, n. n., *reward,*
recompense.
quemadmŏdum, adv., *how, in*
what manner.
debeo, debui, debĭtum, v. a. 2,
am bound, ought, should.

37.

praepăro, v. a. 1, *make ready*
beforehand, prepare, provide.
tempto, v. a. 1, *try, test.*
quisnam,quaenam,quidnam,in-
terrog.pron.,*who,which,what.*
dimīco, v. n. 1, *fight, contend.*
infĕr-us, -a, -um, adj., *that is*
below, underneath, lower,
comp., inferior; superl.,
infĭmus.

rad-ix, -Icis, n. f., *root, foot* of a mountain.
semper, adv., *always.*
elĭcio, elĭcĕre, elicui and elexi, elĭcitum, v. a. 3, *draw out, entice out.*
commŏd-us, -a, -um, adj., *fit, suitable, proper.*
insolĭt-us, -a, -um, adj., *unaccustomed.*
cotidiăn-us, -a, -um, adj., *of every day, daily.*
defatĭgo, v. a. 1, *weary out.*
consuetŭd-o, -ĭnis, n. f., *custom.*
tunc, adv., *then.*
diffĕro, differre, distŭli, dilătum, v. a. irreg., *put off, defer, postpone.*
inquam, v. defect., *say.*
nos, nostrum, nobis, pl. of ego, *we.*
facĭlĕ, adv., *easily.*
confestim, adv., *immediately, forthwith.*

38.

satis, adv., *enough.*
praedīco, praedixi, praedictum, v. a. 3, *say beforehand, order.*
impĕt-us, -ûs, n. m., *attack, onset.*
neve or neu, adv., *and not, nor.*
distrăho, distraxi, distractum, v. a. 3, *pull asunder, separate, break up, disorder.*
patior, pati, passus sum, v. dep. 3, *suffer, allow, permit.*
infest-us, -a, -um, adj., *hostile;* infestis pilis, *with javelins poised or levelled.*
pil-um, -i, n. n., *javelin.*

concurro, concurri, concursum, v. n. 3, *rush together, join battle.*
us-us, -ûs, n. m., *use, experience.*
exercĭtăt-us, -a, -um, part. adj., *well exercised, practised, trained.*
sponte, an abl., *in good prose always joined with meă, tuă, suă;* sua sponte, *of their own accord, of themselves.*
curs-us, -ûs, n. m., *running, course, speed, charge.*
reprĭmo, repressi, repressum, v. a. 3, *check, restrain.*
renŏvo, v. a. 1, *renew.*
praecĭpio, praecĭpĕre, praecēpi, praeceptum, v. a. 3, *admonish, enjoin, order.*
gladi-us, -i, n. m., *sword.*
stringo, strinxi, strictum, v. a. 3, *draw, unsheath.*
tel-um, -i, n. n., *missile, dart.*

39.

sinist-er, -ra, -rum, adj., *left, on the left.*
corn-u, -ûs, n. n., *horn, wing (of an army).*
univers-us, -a, -um, adj., *all together.*
lăt-us, -ĕris, n. n., *side, flank.*
apert-us, -a, -um, part. adj., *open, exposed, unprotected.*
solum, adv., *alone, only.*
protĭnus, adv., *forthwith, immediately.*
recens, recentis, adj., *fresh.*
succĕdo, successi, successum, v. n. 3, *come into the place of, relieve, replace.*

40.

pello, pepŭli, pulsum, v. a. 3, *rout, drive back, discomfit.*

equ-us, -i, n. m., *horse.*

event-us, -ūs, n. m., *issue, result.*

industriē, adv., *diligently, rigorously.*

diu, adv., *long;* comp., diutius; superl., diutissime : quam diutissime, *as long as possible.*

intra, prep. gov. acc., *within.*

versor, v. dep. 1, *move about in a place, am in.*

detrăho, detraxi, detractum, v. a. 3, *strip off, remove.*

insign-e, -is, n. n., *mark, badge, decoration.*

decumān-us, -a, -um, adj., *of the tenth cohort ;* porta decumana, the main entrance of a Roman camp, placed the farthest from the enemy, opposite the porta praetoria. It was so called because the tenth cohort of each legion was there encamped.

ēĭcio, eĭcĕre, eiēci, eiectum, v. a. 3, *cast out, expel ;* se eicere, *to burst out, rush out, sally forth.*

citāt-us, -a, -um, part. adj., *urged on, rapid ;* equo citato, *at full gallop.*

Larīs-a, -ae, n. f., a city in Thessaly on the Peneus, now Larissa.

41.

persĕquor, persĕcūtus or persequutus sum, v. dep. 3, *pursue, follow up.*

edict-um, -i, n. n., *a proclamation.*

nom-en, -ĭnis, n. n., *name.*

Amphipŏl-is, -is, n. f., a city in Macedonia, on the Strymon.

iuvĕn-is, adj., *young ;* comp. iunior.

iuro, v. n. 1, *swear, take an oath.*

utrum ... an, *whether ... or.*

suspici-o, -ōnis, n. f., *suspicion.*

long-us, -a, -um, adj., *long.*

occulto, v. a. 1, *hide, conceal.*

ancŏr-a, -ae, n. f., *anchor.*

voco, v. a. 1, *call.*

hosp-es, -ĭtis, n. m., *friend.*

sumpt-us, -ūs, n. m., *expense, charge.*

corrŏgo, v. a. 1, *bring together by entreaty, collect.*

Mytilēn-ae, -arum, n. f. pl., *Mytilene,* the capital of Lesbos.

retĭneo, retinui, retentum, v. a. 3, *hold back, detain.*

addo, addĭdi, addĭtum, v. a. 3, *add.*

actuari-us, -a, -um, adj., *swift.*

Cilici-a, -ae, n. f., a province in the southern part of Asia Minor.

Cypr-us, -i, n. f., an island off the coast of Asia Minor.

consens-us, -ūs, n. m., *agreement, consent.*

Antiochens-es, -ium, n. m., the inhabitants of Antiochia.

illic, adv., *there.*

negotior, v. dep. 1, *carry on business, trade.*

arx, arcis, n. f., *citadel.*

F

exclūdo, exclūsi, exclusum, v. a. 3, *shut out, exclude.*
Antiochī-a, -ae, n. f., *Antioch.*

42.

Syrī-a, -ae, n. f., *Syria.*
aes, aeris, n. n., *copper, bronze, money.*
pond-us, -ĕris, n. n., *weight.*
impōno, impōsui, impŏsĭtum, v. a. 3, *put on board ship.*
armo, v. a. 1, *furnish with arms, arm, equip.*
Pelusi-um, -i, n. n., *a city at the eastern mouth of the Nile, now Tineh.*
Ptolemae-us, -i, n. m., *Ptolemy,* the son of Ptolemy Auletes. By his father's will he was to reign jointly with his sister Cleopatra, with whom however he was now at war.
pu-er, -ĕri, n. m., *boy.*
aet-as, -ātis, n. f., *age.*
sor-or, -ōris, n. f., *sister.*
Cleopatr-a, -ae, n. f., Cleopatra, queen of Egypt and daughter of Ptolemy Auletes.
propinqu-us, -i, n. m., *relative, kinsman.*
amīc-us, -i, n. m., *friend.*
expello, expŭli, expulsum, v. a. 3, *drive out, expel.*
hospiti-um, -i, n.n., *hospitality, friendly relation.*
pat-er, -ris, n. m., *father.*
Alexandrī-a, -ae, n. f., a city of Egypt.

ops, opis, n. f., *might, strength;* pl., *wealth, resources, influence.*
calamĭt-as, -ātis, n. f., *mis fortune, calamity, adversity.*
tego, texi, tectum, v. a. 3, *cover, shelter, protect.*
procurati-o, -ōnis, n. f., *charge, administration.*
sollicĭto, v. a. 1, *agitate, rouse, incite.*
regi-us, -a, -um, adj., *of or belonging to a king, royal.*
Aegypt-us, -i, n. f., *Egypt.*
despĭcio, despicĕre, despexi, despectum, v. a. 3, *look down upon, despise.*
plerumque, adv., *for the most part, commonly.*
existo, exstĭti, exstĭtum, v. n. 3, *come forth, spring from.*
liberalĭter, adv., *courteously, graciously.*
Achill-as, -ae, n. m., *Achillas.*
singulār-is, -e, adj., *singular, remarkable, matchless.*
audaci-a, -ae, n. f., *boldness, daring.*
Septimi-us, -i, n. m., a Roman gentile name.
notitĭ-a, -ae, n. f., *knowledge, acquaintance with.*
praed-o, -ōnis, n. m., *pirate, robber.*
navicŭl-a, -ae, n. f., *a small ship, boat, skiff.*
parvŭl-us, -a, -um, adj., *very small.*

NOTES.

1.

litterae. In this letter Caesar offered to lay down all his commands if Pompey would do the same.

consulibus. The consuls were C. Claudius Marcellus and L. Cornelius Lentulus Crus.

in eandem sententiam, *to the same purport.*

Scipio. Q. Caecilius Metellus Pius Scipio, whose daughter, Cornelia, Pompey married in B.C. 52.

Pompeio is dat., *that it is Pompey's purpose.*

2.

ad vesperum. The Senate could not legally continue to deliberate after sunset.

evocantur. The Senate was summoned to the Temple of Bellona, outside the walls, to give audience to Pompey, who could not legally enter the city without laying down his military command.

infirmiores, *somewhat wavering, inclined to waver.* The comparative is often used without any direct idea of comparison to express *somewhat, rather, too.*

3.

rem ad arma deduci, he was eager *that the question should be brought to the arbitrament of war.*

ne quid respublica detrimenti capiat, *that the State sustain no injury.* The gen. **detrimenti** depends on **quid,** *anything, aught of injury.*

Ravennae, *at Ravenna,* locative case.

63

4.

eadem, etc., *makes the same proposals which he had communicated through Scipio.*

tota Italia, abl.

5.

Ariminum, *to Ariminum*, acc. of motion to a place. To reach Ariminum Caesar had to cross the river Rubicon and leave his province. This act was virtually a declaration of war. Plutarch, Suetonius, and Lucan represent Caesar as pausing on the bank of the river, anxiously pondering on the probable results of the course he was about to take, and finally announcing his decision to cross in the words "The die is cast." Caesar himself mentions no such incident.

M. Antonium. This was Shakespeare's Mark Antony.

Arretium, *to Arretium.*

Arimini, *at Ariminum.*

duabus, supply cohortibus.

6.

Romam, lit. *to Rome*, acc. of motion to a place, because the news was brought *to* Rome. The English expression is, announced *at Rome.*

invasit, such a panic *fell on* (the city), the object of the verb being omitted.

citra Capuam, *on this* (that is, on the Roman) *side of Capua.*

Capuae, *at Capua.*

7.

Asculum Picenum. *Asculum in Picenum*, to be distinguished from Asculum in Apulia. **Picenum** is here an adj.

decem cohortibus, instrumental ablative.

Corfinium. *to Corfinium.*

unum diem, *during one day*, acc. of duration of time.

ad oppidum, *near, in the neighbourhood of the town.*

8.

qui petant, sends persons *to beg,* lit., *who may beg.*

sese rem in summum, etc., *that he would not bring matters to a crisis.*

id ne fieri posset obsidione ... fiebat. *this had become impossible owing to the blockade,* etc.

cum paucis familiaribus, *with a few who were his intimates.*

consilium fugae capere, *make arrangements for flight.*

sacramentum apud se dicere, *swear allegiance to him.*

9.

Brundisium proficiscitur, *sets out for Brundisium,* acc. of motion to a place.

Brundisii, *at Brundisium.*

Italiā, abl., depart *from Italy.*

ad spem, *for the hope* of finishing the business.

10.

cum postulavisset, his forbearance *in* voluntarily *demanding* that the armies should be disbanded.

docet, *he points out.*

in se, *in their own case.*

mitti oportere, *should be sent.*

Romae, *at Rome.*

13.

contenditur proelio, *a battle is fought,* lit., it is contended in battle.

superiores discessisse, *had come off with the advantage, had got the best of the fight.*

14.

suis locis, *in a region favourable to themselves, on their own ground.*

positum, *situated.*

16.

prima luce, *at daybreak.*

praesidio castris, double dat., *for the defence of the camp.*

numero iumentorum, etc.   The beasts of burden were stationed in the river to break the force of the current, and so make it safer for the foot soldiers to cross.

17.

nihil negotii. *no trouble, an easy task.*

18.

iri videbatur, impers. pass., translate, *they seemed to be going.*

superare regionem castrorum, when they perceived that the foremost men *were passing beyond the line of the camp.*   The camp of Afranius lay between Caesar and the defile leading to the Ebro.   By the detour over the rough ground Caesar brought his men to a point somewhat nearer the defile than that occupied by Afranius, before the latter perceived the object of the manœuvre.

conclamatur ad arma, *the cry, to arms! is raised.*

ex magnis rupibus, *after the great cliffs.*

19.

in eam spem venerat, etc., *had conceived the hope that.* etc.

premebantur pabulatione, *suffered from the difficulty of getting forage.*

explicitius (consilium), *the simpler* (plan).

quo spatio, etc., *and in such a distance they perceived that the undertaking might be liable to more mischances.*

pugnatur acriter, *there is a fierce fight.*

venitur, impers. pass., translate, *they come.*

20.

neque se in ullam partem movebat, *and yet did not take either side.*

ad Massiliam, *at Marseilles.*

se ad motus fortunae movere coepit, *he began to change
with the changes of fortune.*

Gades, *to Gades.*

Gadibus, *from Gades.*

21.

ipso, Varro *himself.*

Hispalim, *to Hispalis.*

Italicam, *to Italica.*

Sextum Caesarem. This was Sextus Julius Caesar, grand-
son of Caesar's uncle.

biduum, *for two days,* acc. of duration of time.

Cordubae, *at Corduba.*

22.

duabus ex partibus, *on two sides.*

23.

huic simultas cum Curione intercedebat, *between him and
Curio enmity existed.*

quod tribunus plebis, *because (Curio) when tribune,* etc.

prima nocte, *at the beginning of the night.*

24.

rem gestam cognovit, *he learned of the engagement that had
taken place.*

ut defessis, *considering how weary they were.*

25.

Cn. Domitius. This was Cn. Domitius Calvinus, a supporter
of Caesar, who is also mentioned in **34.** He must not be
confounded with Caesar's opponent L. Domitius Ahenobarbus,
who is mentioned in **7, 8, 22.**

in Caesaris conspectum, *into Caesar's presence.*

ad unum omnes, *all to a man, without exception.*

ad officium imperiumque, *in obedience to duty and orders.*

hoc timore, *by fear of this,* lit., *by this fear.*

adire tardarentur, *were hindered from approaching.*

Varum. P. Attius Varus was a partisan of Pompey, and was assisted by Juba in opposing Curio.

legatorum numero, *as envoys.*

26.

consules, etc. Caesar had been consul with Bibulus in . 59 B.C., and was therefore again eligible in 48 B.C., after the lapse of ten years.

angustior, *somewhat weakened.*

ambitûs, gen. case.

27.

tantum navium, (only) *so many ships,* that is, *so few.*

Dyrrhachii, *at Dyrrhachium.*

Apolloniae, *at Apollonia.*

transire prohiberet, *prevent* Caesar *from crossing* the sea.

eius rei causâ, *for that purpose.*

omnibus ad unam. Compare, ad unum omnes, in **25.**

28.

offenderunt, *came to grief.*

Corcyrae, *at Corcyra.*

inanibus, supply navibus, the *empty* ships.

29.

ad extremum auxilium descenderunt, *had recourse to the last resource.*

30.

idoneum ... quem ... mitteret, *a fit person for him to send.*

31.

Dyrrhachio timens, *fearing for Dyrrhachium.*

32.

multi iam menses erant. *many months were now past.*

Brundisio, *from Brundisium.*

33.

Dyrrhachium compelli, *be driven into Dyrrhachium.*

primum agmen, *the vanguard.*

34.

prima nocte, *early in the night.*

de quarta vigilia, *in the fourth night-watch.*

castris Scipionis castra collata, *his camp close to that of Scipio.*

subiecta Candaviae, *close to the border of Candavia.*

obiectum Thessaliae, *lying opposite, facing, Thessaly,* that is, a frontier town of Thessaly.

35.

venientibus, *for persons coming, as one comes* from Epirus.

collatâ fortunâ, abl. abs.

36.

tardius aut consideratius, *somewhat slowly or deliberately.*

servorum numero habere, *treat or regard as slaves.*

37.

quidnam propositi aut voluntatis, *what plan or inclination.*

extra cotidianam consuetudinem, *departing from the daily custom.*

38.

It is to be observed that Caesar makes no mention of Pharsalus or Pharsalia in connexion with the celebrated battle here described. The title " Battle of Pharsalia " is first found in the History of the Alexandrian War, commonly attributed to A. Hirtius, an officer of Caesar's.

tantum spatii, *so much space.*

neve se loco moverent, *and not stir from their position.*

non concurri, impers. pass., *that a rush to the encounter was not made* by Pompey's men.

consumptis viribus, *with exhausted strength.*

exceperunt, *they parried.*

39.

loco motus, *driven from their position.*

infestis signis, *with hostile standards*, **that is, in** *fighting array.*

se loco tenuerat, *had remained in position.*

40.

acie excessit, *left the battle-field.*

equo, *on horseback.*

summae rei diffidens, *distrustful of the ultimate issue.*

41.

ad ancoram constitit, *lay at anchor.*

42.

pro hospitio atque amicitia patris. It was partly through Pompey's influence that Ptolemy Auletes was restored by A. Gabiuius after his expulsion by the Alexandrians.

EXERCISES.

1.

1. Caesar's letter.
2. To Lentulus the consul.
3. Of the same opinion.
4. By the speech (abl.) of Scipio.
5. Pompey did not fail the commonwealth.
6. Caesar sent a letter.

2.

1. The power of the senate.
2. To all the enemies of Caesar.
3. The cries of the centurions.
4. The enemies of Pompey will be frightened.
5. Pompey will praise his kinsmen.
6. He collected the enemies of Caesar.

3.

1. The commonwealth will not sustain injury.
2. The tribune will take to flight.
3. He will be reconciled to his enemy.
4. They will await an answer.
5. Caesar will send (mitto) moderate demands.
6. The friendship of the consuls.

4.

1. The general will make a speech in the presence of the senate.
2. The thirteenth legion will be present.
3. The soldiers repelled their wrongs.
4. Caesar learned these things.
5. On the next day Pompey delivered a speech outside the city.
6. He recounted the same things.

5.

1. The legion set out for Ancona.
2. He ordered the rest of the soldiers to follow closely.
3. The winter quarters were at Pisaurum.
4. Caesar set out with the soldiers.
5. He occupied Ariminum and Fanum with a legion each.
6. He learned the inclination of the soldiers themselves.

6.

1. At Rome terror suddenly fell on (invado) all.
2. The consuls fled from the city.
3. Marcellus followed his colleague.
4. All things on this side of Capua seem safe.
5. Pompey had received two (duo) legions from Caesar.
6. He announced these things (neut. pl. of hic) at Rome.

7.

1. The cohorts of Lentulus held the town.
2. He heard of the arrival of Caesar.
3. The soldiers fell in with the cohort of Rufus.
4. They came by forced marches to Asculum.
5. The soldiers delayed ten days at Corfinium.
6. Caesar will pitch his camp near the wall of the town.

8.

1. Men acquainted with the country were sent to Pompey.
2. They begged that he should help them.
3. He ordered all the forces to come to him.
4. Domitius provided for his own safety.
5. The soldiers sent envoys from (e) the camp.
6. They sent away the envoy unharmed.

9.

1. The consul will set out with the army for Dyrrhachium.
2. Twenty cohorts will remain at Brindisi.
3. Pompey's soldiers embarked and set sail.
4. Although he feared delay, he did not follow Pompey.
5. He did not give up the plan of setting out for Spain.
6. He collected ships and crossed the sea.

10.

1. The soldiers were quartered in the free towns.
2. Caesar assembled the senate.

3. Owing to fear envoys were not sent to Pompey.

4. Caesar spent the next days at Rome in vain.

5. Those who approved the matter remained voluntarily at Rome.

6. The soldiers when departing (*use* part.) recounted their wrongs.

11.

1. Pompey's lieutenants were holding Spain.

2. Of these lieutenants one was defending Hither Spain, the second Further Spain, and the third was in Lusitania.

3. Petreius had an equal number of legions.

4. Varro sent forward the soldiers that (qui) he had.

12.

1. They made a bridge over the river.

2. The cavalry of Caesar came thither.

3. Caesar cut off Afranius from all supplies.

4. The town and the river were two miles distant from one another.

13.

1. The soldiers, hoping for this, ran forward to the same hill.

2. Afranius sent a cohort by a short cut (*say* by a shorter way).

3. Those who came first to the hill compelled the enemy to take to flight.

4. Afranius thought he had come off best in the battle because our men took to flight in the first encounter.
5. Afterwards (postea) our men drove the enemy into the city.
6. He ordered the soldiers of the ninth legion to halt under the wall.

14.

1. Many men of Osca promised to carry out (*say* to do) his commands.
2. They transferred the seat of war (*say simply* the war) to Celtiberia.
3. Winter was now approaching (appropinquo), and he led his army across the river Hiberus.
4. They made two bridges of boats.
5. Those who bordered on the river revolted from Afranius.
6. The town was two miles distant from the river Sicoris.

15.

1. Caesar will make a ford across (*say* in) the river Sicoris.
2. He was able to turn aside some part of the river.
3. The cavalry dared to cross the river.
4. The depth of the water was so great that (tantus ut) the infantry could not cross.

5. Accordingly the cavalry harassed the rear of the army.
6. The soldiers hampered the march of their enemies.

16.

1. They informed Caesar that the army was ready to cross the river.
2. Many soldiers feared the great size of the river.
3. He left as a guard for the camp the soldiers whose spirit was wavering.
4. He placed many beasts of burden in the river at the spot where he was about to lead across his soldiers.
5. He did not expose his army to the swiftness of the river.
6. At dawn (*say* at the first light) he led forth the soldiers lightly equipped.

17.

1. The centurions halted that they might not (that not = ne) expose the soldiers to battle while wearied.
2. All those who examined the nature of the place reported the same thing.
3. Next day the enemy seized the pass.
4. About midnight the general again tried to advance.
5. The signal being given (abl. abs.) the army set out earlier than the general had ordered.
6. Caesar pitched his camp on a lofty (editus) hill.

16.

1. All Caesar's forces marched to the Ebro by a great round.
2. There was no regular (certus) road by which he might lead the army.
3. There was a contest of speed between (inter) the two armies.
4. Caesar's soldiers were the first to complete (*say* first completed) the march.
5. The enemy halted on certain hills.
6. Our men followed them with insulting cries.

19.

1. There is hope that a successful battle may be fought (*say* of fighting a successful battle).
2. A great number of the enemy formed the hope (*say* came into this hope) of deserting to Caesar (*say* that they could [acc. and inf.] desert).
3. Caesar replied that he had formed the hope of finishing the matter without a battle.
4. The enemy could not any longer (diutius) bear their suffering.
5. Many soldiers of the rear-guard were killed.
6. They are suffering want of everything, because they pitched their camp in an unfavourable spot.

20.

1. Varro, who at first (primo) spoke in a very friendly way about Caesar, afterwards prepared for war.

2. For he learned that large reinforcements had assembled at (*say* to) Massilia.
3. When the things that had been done in Italy were known (abl. abs.), a levy of troops was held in Spain.
4. The cohorts that were in garrison at Gades secured the city for Caesar.
5. All the chief men of Gades were there.
6. Accordingly he betook himself to Gades with all his army.

21.

1. While Varro looked on, his soldiers broke up the camp and retired to Seville.
2. The soldiers were informed that the gates of the city were shut against them.
3. Caesar appointed Sextus to the command of the legion.
4. When Caesar came to Cadiz he thanked the magistrates and the chief men of the state.
5. He there learned that Lepidus was praetor.
6. The magistrates ordered the soldiers to remain at Cordova for two days.

22.

1. While Trebonius had charge of (praesum with dat.) the siege, many mantlets and towers were advanced against the town.

2. So great was the force of the engines that no mantlet could withstand them.
3. There was a great scarcity of provisions at Marseilles.
4. Those who had surrendered, afterwards brought forth all their arms from the town.
5. Domitius ordered his men (sui) to go on board the ships which he had provided.
6. The stormy weather was a help (say for a help) to those who were setting out (use part.).

23.

1. Through a long continuance of peace men become (fio) unfamiliar with war.
2. Certain deserters said that the king had come.
3. Juba killed a great number of those who had confiscated his kingdom.
4. The messengers said that the enemy were approaching.
5. At the beginning of the night the Numidians attacked the camp.
6. Trusting the deserters, they rashly ventured on an engagement (say committed the matter to a battle).

24.

1. Being informed about the engagement that had taken place (res gesta) they went forth from the camp.

2. They set out at the third (tertius) watch and advanced three miles (*say* having set out advanced, *omitting* and).
3. Not even the cavalry were able to follow.
4. In the battle by night courage neither failed the general (dux) as being weary, nor the soldiers as being exhausted with toil.
5. Saburra ordered the soldiers to lead the elephants down to the plain.
6. Juba and Saburra trusted chiefly to their elephants.

25.

1. The king sent auxiliaries to (*say* who should, qui with subj.) increase the forces.
2. At the same time many left the battle-array because they had received wounds.
3. Curio declared that he would never seek safety by flight after the loss of his army (*say* his army having been lost, abl abs.).
4. Those who returned from the battle went on board a few skiffs.
5. A great part of those whom Juba did not put to death he declared to be his booty.
6. Many skiffs did not approach nearer, lest they should be sunk by the multitude of the cavalry.

26.

1. The fear of the cancelling of debts commonly (fere) follows civil war.

2. That he might remove this fear, Caesar ordered a valuation of property to be made.
3. He likewise restored to their former state those who had been condemned by Pompey.
4. He ordered the debtors to pay to their creditors the sums of money that had been lent (creditae pecuniae).
5. Arbitrators made a valuation of all possessions.
6. When Caesar had resigned the dictatorship he set out for Brundisium.

27.

1. Thither came twelve legions and all the cavalry.
2. But Caesar found few (pauci) ships, so that he could not transport all the soldiers.
3. Pompey collected a large fleet in order that he might cross the sea and winter at Dyrrhachium.
4. Six hundred men set sail and reached land the following day.
5. They found a safe (tutus) roadstead between the island (insula) and the coast.
6. The soldiers were landed between Apollonia and Buthrotum.

28.

1. At night the same ships set sail for Brundisium.
2. But Bibulus ordered them all to be set on fire, and the sailors to be put to death.

3. The business was completed by Bibulus, who afterwards, availing himself (usus) of the night
breeze, returned to land.

29.

1. The five camps, with which the town was sur-
rounded, were defended by their situation
(*say* by the nature of the place).
2. The citizens freed the town from (*use* libero with
acc. and abl.) blockade by the help of slaves.
3. At noon Octavius began to attack the town, but
he was compelled by the citizens to flee for
refuge to the ships.
4. On account of their small numbers (paucitas), when
winter was now approaching, they betook themselves to Pompey.

30.

1. Caesar sent messages to Pompey who was in winter
quarters at Apollonia.
2. At the same time he set out for Oricum with all
his troops.
3. Those who were in command of the town, opened
the gates and surrendered to Caesar.
4. And when he had come thither (*say* whither when
he had come), he began to advance on (petere)
Apollonia by forced marches.

31.

1. But Pompey was said to be advancing thither, marching day and night.
2. He ordered the legions, whose arrival he had awaited, to winter there under canvas.
3. Accordingly (itaque) they laid out a camp by the river Apsus.
4. All the forces that (qui) Pompey had brought together did the same thing.

32.

1. About the same time Caesar learned that some legions had come from Brindisi.
2. Pompey adopted the plan of attacking (say that he should attack) the soldiers on the march.
3. He posted his forces in a suitable place in order that he might attack the enemy from an ambush on their arrival (use part.).
4. Pompey kept his forces in camp all day, that his design might be the better concealed.
5. Having found a suitable harbour, he ran his ships in thither.
6. They had neglected no opportunity of sailing.

33.

1. Accordingly they both set out for the same place next day.
2. Scouts informed Pompey that the enemy had moved their camp.

3. Caesar hoped that he could reach Dyrrhachium in the morning by a short cut.
4. When the ships were seen at a distance, the people of Apollonia (Apolloniates) thought they must adopt another plan.
5. The soldiers of Caesar bore toil cheerfully.
6. Pompey was cut off from the town to which (*say* whither, quo) he had brought together all his supplies.

34.

1. Caesar being baffled in his earlier design changed his whole plan of war and set out for Apollonia.
2. Pompey also hastened into Macedonia that he might attack Domitius.
3. But Caesar bore help to Domitius, fearing lest he should be exposed to danger.
4. Being informed by (per) scouts of the arrival of Pompey, he avoided the enemy.
5. When he had sent all his baggage forward to the town, he marched thither himself with all speed.
6. He was unexpectedly informed that Caesar had set out (*say* about the setting out of Caesar).

35.

1. On the same day that Caesar came to Gomphi he attacked the walls of the town.

2. The soldiers carried the town by storm and forth-with plundered it.

3. The people of Larissa were restrained by Scipio from opening their gates to Caesar.

4. He found the fields full of corn (*use* pl.), which the people of Gomphi said was nearly ripe.

36.

1. All things increased the hope of victory to such a degree that the soldiers of Pompey were now discussing their rewards.

2. Pompey thanked all the army and received both Scipio's soldiers and his own into one camp.

3. He was so pleased with authority that he did not share his honour with the ex-consuls.

4. He treated as slaves those with whom he ought to have shared his honours.

37.

1. Pompey could not be enticed out to battle because (quod) he considered the place to be unfavourable.

2. He drew up his army at the foot of the mountain that he might seem to be ready for fighting.

3. He advanced a long distance from the stockade in order that he might weary out the army of the enemy.

4. They did not easily find an opportunity of fighting.
5. When it was noticed that the enemy had advanced far from the camp, Caesar gave the signal for setting out.
6. He postponed his march and drew up his army in battle array.

38.

1. Pompey's men did not move from their position, but received the charge of our men, as Pompey had ordered.
2. Caesar did not order his men to check their course, but of their own accord they halted when they perceived a charge was not made by the enemy.
3. Caesar directed that they should hurl their javelins and afterwards quickly draw their swords.
4. And when the soldiers perceived this (*say* which things when, quae cum), they charged into the space that lay (*say* was) between the two lines of battle.

39.

1. The cavalry made an attack upon our line on the exposed flank.
2. When Caesar perceived this he ordered fresh men to take the place of those who were weary.
3. Six cohorts attacked the left wing in rear so that they could not withstand the attack.

4. Those who up to that time withstood every attack, took to flight and made for the mountains.

40.

1. Pompey put his chief trust in his cavalry, and when he saw that they were routed he fled for refuge to the camp.
2. He had left there certain cohorts as a garrison.
3. When the enemy were now within the stockade, those who were defending the camp burst forth from the decuman gate and made for Larissa at full gallop.
4. With the same speed a few others, having found horses, reached the sea by a night journey.

41.

1. Caesar pursued Pompey because he seemed (videor) to be again mustering forces and making fresh levies.
2. During two days he concealed his plan and lay at anchor.
3. No one could judge whether he had set out for Mytilene or was attempting to renew the war.
4. Many Romans go to Antioch to carry on business there.
5. When they heard that the citadel had been taken they left the place.

42.

1. Pompey abandoned the design of visiting Syria when he learned these things.
2. Cleopatra, the sister of King Ptolemy, was now carrying on war and had come to Pelusium.
3. She was trying (conor) to drive Ptolemy from the kingdom and had pitched her camp at no great distance from his.
4. Septimius from being a friend became an enemy, and along with Achillas, a man of conspicuous daring, put Pompey to death.

INDEX.

appello (appellāre), 23.
appello (appellĕre), 23.
appropinquo, 23.
Apsus, 31.
aptus, 26.
apud, 4.
Apulia, 6.
aqua, 15.
aquor, 19.
arbiter, 26.
arbitror, 24.
arcano, 8.
Ariminum, 5.
arma, 3.
armo, 42.
Arretium, 5.
arx, 41.
Asculum, 7.
Asparagium, 32.
asper, 17.
at, 24.
atque, 2.
attingo, 14.
auctor, 23.
auctoritas, 30.
auctus, see augeo. 25.
audacia, 42.
audeo, 15.
audio, 19.
augeo, 25.
aura, 28.
Ausetani, 14.
auster, 32.
aut, 16.
autem, 13.
auxilium, 14.
averto, 3.

Bagrada, 23.

bellum, 14.
bene, 19.
beneficium, 30.
Bibulus, 28.
biduum, 21.
bis, 22.
brevis, 13.
Brundisinus, 9.
Brundisium, 9.

C., 1.
Caesar, 1.
Calagurritani, 14.
calamitas, 42.
Calenus, 32.
campester, 17.
campus, 17.
Candavia, 30.
capio, 3.
Capua, 6.
carpo, 15.
Cassius, 21.
castra, 7.
Castulonensis, 11.
casus, 19.
causa, 3.
cedo, 24.
celeritas, 18.
celeriter, 11.
Celtiberia, 14.
centuria, 16.
centurio, 2.
Ceraunii, 27.
cerno, 33.
certamen, 18.
certus, 16.
Cilicia, 41.
circiter, 17.
circuitus, 18.
circumcludo, 32.
circumdo, 25.
circumeo, 24.

circummunio, 23.
circumunmunitio, 8.
citatus, 40.
citerior, 11.
citra, 6.
civilis, 26.
civis, 27.
civitas, 14.
clam, 32.
clamor, 17.
classis, 27.
Cleopatra, 42.
Cn., 6.
coactus, see cogo, 2.
coepi 20.
cogito, 14.
cognitus, see cognosco, 4.
cognosco, 4.
cogo, 2.
cohors, 5.
cohortor, 13.
collega, 6.
colligo, 6.
collis, 12.
colloco, 32.
colloquium, 19.
colloquor, 8.
comitium, 26.
commeatus, 12.
commemoro, 4.
committo, 23.
commodus, 37.
commoror, 21.
communio, 12.
communis, 3.
commutatio, 14.
commuto, 34.
comparo, 22.
compello, 13.
compleo, 2.
complures, 19.

H

occasio, 19.
occasus, 35.
occulte, 17.
occulto, 41.
occultus, 32.
occupo, 5.
occurro, 28.
Octavius, 29.
Octogesa, 14.
offendo, 28.
officium, 11.
omitto, 9.
omnia, n. pl. of
  omnis, 2.
omnis, 2.
onus, 17.
opera, 3.
opinio, 13.
oportet, 10.
oppidum, 7.
oppono, 18.
oppugnatio, 22.
oppugno, 29.
ops, 42.
opus, 9.
ora, 27.
oratio, 1.
ordo, 2.
Oricum, 30.
oro, 8.
os, 1.
Oscenses, 14.
ostendo, 4.
otiosus, 27.
otium, 23.

P., 26.
pabulatio, 19.
Palaeste, 27.
palam, 23.
par, 11.
paratus, 4.

pareo, 35.
paro, 20.
pars, 9.
partior, 11.
parvus, 33.
passus (subst.), 12.
pater, 42.
patientia, 10.
patior, 38.
pauci, 8.
paucitas, 29.
paulatim, 18.
paulo, 12.
paulum, 19.
pecunia, 4.
pedes, 15.
pellis, 31.
pello, 40.
Pelusium, 42.
per, 4.
perficio, 26.
perfuga, 23.
perfugio, 19.
periculosus, 27.
periculum, 8.
peritus, 8.
permoveo, 9.
perpauci, 25.
perpetior, 19.
perscribo, 20.
persequor, 41.
perspicio, 17.
perterreo, 21.
pertineo, 18.
perturbo, 30.
pervenio, 7.
pes, 24.
pestilentia, 22.
peto, 8.
Petra, 33.
Petreius, 11.
Picenus, 7.

pilum, 38.
Pisaurum, 5.
planities, 18.
plebs, 3.
plenus, 35.
plerique, 2.
plerumque, 42.
plures, see multus, 14.
polliceor, 1.
Pompeianus, 20.
Pompeius (proper name and adj.), 1
pondus, 42.
pono, 7.
pons, 12.
porta, 8.
portus, 9.
positus, see pono, 7.
possessio, 26.
possum, 8.
post, 14.
postea, 20.
posterum, 2.
posterus, 2.
postquam, 33.
postremo, 36.
postridie, 27.
postulatum, 3.
postulo, 10.
potestas, 2.
potissimum, 25.
praecipio, 38.
praecipito, 32.
praecludo, 21.
praeda, 25.
praedico, 38.
praedico, 25.
praedo, 42.
praefero, 13.
praefectus, 23.
praeficio, 21.

traduco, 14.
trans, 31.
transeo, 9.
transfero, 14.
transporto, 27.
Trebonius, 22.
tres, 11.
tribunus, 2.
tribuo, 26.
triginta, 14.
triplex, 12.
tueor, 11.
tum, 15.
tumulus, 12.
tunc, 37.
turbate, 3.
turbidus, 22.
turris, 22.
tutus, 6.

ubi, 12.
ullus, 20.
ulterior, 10.
ultimus, 3.

ultro, 10.
undecim, 26.
universus, 39.
unus, 7.
urbs, 1.
usus (subst.), 38.
ut, 1.
uter, 18.
uterque, 13.
uti, 1.
Utica, 23.
utor, 28.
utrum, 41.

vacuus, 27.
vadum, 15.
vallum, 23.
Varro, 11.
Varus, 25.
vas, 17.
venio, 7.
ventus, 32.
vereor, 17.
vero, 2.

versor, 40.
verto, 13.
vesper, 2.
Vettones, 11.
Vibullius, 7.
victoria, 36.
video, 1.
vigilia, 15.
viginti, 9.
vimen, 22.
vinco, 19.
vinea, 22.
vires, see vis, 16.
virtus, 24.
vis, 16.
viso, 18.
vito, 34.
vivus, 8.
vix, 34.
voco, 41.
voluntas, 5.
vox, 2.
vulnus, 19.

Works on Latin and Greek Grammar and Composition.

LATIN.

Macmillan's Latin Course. FIRST PART. By A. M. Cook, M.A., Assistant Master at St. Paul's School. Gl. 8vo. 3s 6d.
SECOND PART. By A. M. Cook, M.A., and W. E. P. Pantin, M.A. New and Enlarged Edition. Gl. 8vo. 4s 6d.

Macmillan's Shorter Latin Course. By A. M. Cook, M.A. Abridgment of "Macmillan's Latin Course, First Part." Gl. 8vo. 1s 6d. KEY, for Teachers only. Fcap. 8vo. 4s 6d. [Second Part in preparation.

Macmillan's Latin Reader. A Latin Reader for the Lower Forms in Schools. By H. J. Hardy, M.A., Assistant Master at Winchester. Gl. 8vo. 2s 6d.

First Latin Grammar. By M. C. Macmillan, M.A. Fcap. 8vo. 1s 6d.

A Grammar of the Latin Language, from Plautus to Suetonius. By H. J. Roby, M.A., late Fellow of St. John's College, Cambridge. Part I. Sounds, Inflections, Word-formation, Appendices. Cr. 8vo. 9s. Part II. Syntax, Prepositions, etc. 10s 6d.

School Latin Grammar. By the Same. Cr. 8vo. 5s.

Exercises on Latin Syntax and Idiom. Arranged with reference to the above. By E. B. England, Assistant Lecturer at the Owens College, Manchester. Gl. 8vo. 2s. 6d. KEY, for Teachers only. Gl. 8vo. 2s 6d.

An Elementary Latin Grammar. By H. J. Roby, M.A., and Professor A. S. Wilkins, Litt.D. Gl. 8vo. 2s 6d.

Short Exercises in Latin Prose Composition and Examination Papers IN LATIN GRAMMAR Part I. By Rev. H. Belcher, LL.D. Pott 8vo. 1s 6d. KEY, for Teachers only. Pott 8vo. 3s 6d.
Part II. On the Syntax of Sentences, with an Appendix, including Exercises in Latin Idioms, etc. Pott 8vo. 2s. KEY, for Teachers only. Pott 8vo. 3s.

First Lessons in Latin. By K. M. Eicke, B.A., Assistant Master at Oundle School. Gl. 8vo. 2s 6d.

Sermo Latinus. A Short Guide to Latin Prose Composition. By Professor J. P. Postgate, Litt.D., Fellow of Trinity College, Cambridge. Gl. 8vo. 2s 6d. KEY to "Selected Passages." Gl. 8vo. 4s 6d. net.

First Steps to Latin Prose Composition. By Rev. G. Rust, M.A. Pott 8vo. 1s 6d. KEY, for Teachers only. Pott 8vo. 3s 6d.

Latin Prose after the Best Authors: Cæsarian Prose. By F. P. Simpson, B.A. Ex. fcap. 8vo. 2s 6d. KEY, for Teachers only. Gl. 8vo. 5s.

Latin Prose Exercises based upon Cæsar's Gallic War. With a Classification of Cæsar's Chief Phrases and Grammatical Notes on Cæsar's Usages. By Clement Bryans, M.A., Assistant Master at Dulwich College. Gl. 8vo. 2s 6d. KEY, for Teachers only. Gl. 8vo. 4s 6d.

An Introduction to Latin Elegiac Verse Composition. By J. H. Lupton, Sur-Master of St. Paul's School. Gl. 8vo. 2s 6d. KEY TO PART II. (XXV.-C.). Gl. 8vo. 3s 6d.

An Introduction to Latin Lyric Verse Composition. By the Same. Gl. 8vo. 3s. KEY, for Teachers only. Gl. 8vo. 4s 6d.

A First Latin Verse Book. By W. E. P. Pantin, M.A., Assistant Master at St. Paul's School. Gl. 8vo. 1s 6d. KEY, for Teachers only. 4s. net.

Analecta. Selected Passages for Translation. By J. S. Strachan, M.A., Professor of Greek, and A. S. Wilkins, Litt.D., Professor of Latin, Owens College, Manchester. Crown 8vo. Latin Part, 2s 6d. KEY to Latin Passages. Crown 8vo. Sewed, 6d.

MACMILLAN AND CO., LONDON.

Works on Latin and Greek Grammar and Composition.
GREEK.

Macmillan's Greek Course. Edited by Rev. W. G. Rutherford, M.A., LL.D., Headmaster of Westminster. Globe 8vo.
FIRST GREEK GRAMMAR—ACCIDENCE. By the Editor. 2s.
FIRST GREEK GRAMMAR—SYNTAX. By the Same. 2s.
ACCIDENCE AND SYNTAX. In one Volume. 3s 6d.
EASY EXERCISES IN GREEK ACCIDENCE. By H. G. Underhill, M.A., Assistant Master at St. Paul's Preparatory School. 2s.
A SECOND GREEK EXERCISE BOOK. By Rev. W. A. Heard, M.A., Head Master of Fettes College, Edinburgh. 2s 6d.
EASY EXERCISES IN GREEK SYNTAX. By Rev. G. H. Nall, M.A., Assistant Master at Westminster School. 2s 6d.
MANUAL OF GREEK ACCIDENCE. By the Editor. [*In preparation.*]
MANUAL OF GREEK SYNTAX. By the Editor. [*In preparation.*]
ELEMENTARY GREEK COMPOSITION. By the Editor. [*In preparation.*]

Macmillan's Greek Reader. Stories and Legends. A First Greek Reader, with Notes, Vocabulary, and Exercises. By F. H. Colson, M.A., Headmaster of Plymouth College. Globe 8vo. 3s.

First Greek Reader. By Professor John E. B. Mayor, M.A., Fellow of St. John's College, Cambridge. Fcap. 8vo. 4s 6d.

Greek for Beginners. By Rev. J. B. Mayor, M.A., late Professor of Classical Literature in King's College, London. Part I., with Vocabulary. 1s 6d. Parts II. and III., with Vocabulary and Index. Fcap. 8vo. 3s 6d. Complete in one Vol. 4s 6d.

Syntax of the Moods and Tenses of the Greek Verb. By W. W. Goodwin, LL.D., D.C.L., Professor of Greek in Harvard University. New Edition, revised and enlarged. 8vo. 14s.

A Greek Grammar. By the Same. Crown 8vo. 6s.

A Greek Grammar for Schools. By the Same. Crown 8vo. 3s 6d.

First Lessons in Greek. Adapted to Goodwin's Greek Grammar, and designed as an Introduction to the Anabasis of Xenophon. By John Williams White, Assistant Professor of Greek in Harvard University, U.S.A. Cr. 8vo. 3s 6d.

A Greek Grammar for Schools and Colleges. By James Hadley, late Professor in Yale College. Revised by F. de F. Allen, Professor in Harvard College. Crown 8vo. 6s.

A Table of Irregular Verbs, classified according to the arrangement of Curtius's Greek Grammar. By J. M. Marshall, M.A., Headmaster of the Grammar School, Durham. 8vo. 1s.

First Steps to Greek Prose Composition. By Blomfield Jackson, M.A. Pott 8vo. 1s 6d. KEY, for Teachers only. Pott 8vo. 3s 6d.

Second Steps to Greek Prose Composition, with Examination Papers. By the Same. Pott 8vo. 2s 6d. KEY, for Teachers only. Pott 8vo. 3s 6d.

Exercises in the Composition of Greek Iambic Verse. By Rev. H. Kynaston, D.D., Professor of Classics in the University of Durham. With Vocabulary. Ex. fcap. 8vo. 5s. KEY, for Teachers only. Ex. fcap. 8vo. 4s 6d.

Parallel Passages for Translation into Greek and English. With Indexes. By Rev. E. C. Mackie, M.A., Classical Master at Heversham Grammar School. Globe 8vo. 4s 6d.

Analecta Græca. Selected Passages for Translation. By J. S. Strachan, M.A., Professor of Greek, and A. S. Wilkins, Litt.D., Professor of Latin, Owens College, Manchester. Crown 8vo. Greek part, 2s 6d. KEY to Greek Passages. Sewed, 6d.

MACMILLAN AND CO., LONDON.

Works on Latin and Greek Grammar and Composition.
LATIN CLASS BOOKS.

Short Exercises in Latin Prose Composition and Examination Papers IN LATIN GRAMMAR. Part I. By Rev. H. Belcher, LL.D. Pott 8vo. 1s 6d. KEY, for Teachers only. 3s 6d.
Part II. Pott 8vo. 2s. KEY, for Teachers only. Pott 8vo. 3s.

Latin Prose Exercises based upon Cæsar's Gallic War. By Clement Bryans, M.A. Ex. fcap. 8vo. 2s 6d. KEY, for Teachers only. 4s 6d.

First Lessons in Latin. By K. M. Eicke, B.A. Gl. 8vo. 2s 6d.

Exercises on Latin Syntax and Idiom. Arranged with reference to Roby's School Latin Grammar. By E. B. England. Cr. 8vo. 2s. 6d. KEY, for Teachers only. 2s 6d.

An Introduction to Latin Elegiac Verse Composition. By J. H. Lupton, M.A. Gl. 8vo. 2s 6d. KEY TO PART II. (XXV.-C.). Gl. 8vo. 3s 6d.

An Introduction to Latin Lyric Verse Composition. By the Same. Gl. 8vo. 3s. KEY, for Teachers only. Gl. 8vo. 4s 6d.

First Latin Grammar. By M. C. Macmillan, M.A. Fcap. 8vo. 1s 6d.

Macmillan's Latin Course. FIRST PART. By A. M. Cook, M.A., Assistant Master at St. Paul's School. Gl. 8vo. 3s 6d.
SECOND PART. By A. M. Cook, M.A., and W. E. P. Pantin, M.A. New and Enlarged Edition. Gl. 8vo. 4s 6d. [*Third Part in Preparation.*

Macmillan's Latin Reader. A Latin Reader for the Lower Forms in Schools. By H. J. Hardy, M.A. Gl. 8vo. 2s 6d.

Parallel Extracts. Arranged for Translation into English and Latin, with Notes on Idioms. By J. E. Nixon, M.A. Part I. Historical and Epistolary. Crown 8vo. 3s 6d.

Prose Extracts. Arranged for Translation into English and Latin, with General and Special Prefaces on Style and Idiom. By the Same. Second Edition. Crown 8vo. 4s 6d. Selections from the same. 2s 6d.

A First Latin Verse Book. By W. E. P. Pantin, M.A. Gl. 8vo. 1s 6d.

Sermo Latinus. A Short Guide to Latin Prose Composition. By Professor J. P. Postgate, Litt.D. Gl. 8vo. 2s 6d. KEY. Gl. 8vo. 4s 6d. net.

Hints towards Latin Prose Composition. By A. W. Potts, M.A., LL.D. Extra fcap. 8vo. 3s.

Passages for Translation into Latin Prose. Edited with Notes and References to the above. Extra fcap. 8vo. 2s 6d. KEY, for Teachers only. 2s 6d.

Exercises in Latin Verse of Various Kinds. By Rev. G. Preston. Globe 8vo. 2s 6d. KEY, for Teachers only. Globe 8vo. 5s.

A Grammar of the Latin Language, from Plautus to Suetonius. By H. J. Roby, M.A. Part I. Sounds, Inflections, Word-formation, Appendices. Cr. 8vo. 9s. Part II. Syntax, Prepositions, etc. 10s 6d.

School Latin Grammar. By the Same. Cr. 8vo. 5s.

Synthetic Latin Delectus. With Notes and Vocabulary. By E. Rush, B.A. Extra fcap. 8vo. 2s 6d.

First Steps to Latin Prose Composition. By Rev. G. Rust, M.A. Pott 8vo. 1s 6d. KEY, for Teachers only. By W. M. Yates. Pott 8vo. 3s 6d.

Passages from Latin Authors for Translation into English. By E. S. Shuckburgh, M.A. Crown 8vo. 2s.

Latin Prose after the Best Authors: Cæsarian Prose. By F. P. Simpson, B.A. Ex. fcap. 8vo. 2s 6d. KEY, for Teachers only. 5s.

MACMILLAN AND CO., LONDON.

Works on Latin and Greek Grammar and Composition.

GREEK CLASS BOOKS.

Greek and English Dialogues for use in Schools and Colleges. By Prof. J. S. Blackie. New Edition. Fcap. 8vo. 2s 6d.

A Greek Primer, Colloquial and Constructive. Crown 8vo. 2s 6d.

Syntax of the Moods and Tenses of the Greek Verb. By W. W. Goodwin, LL.D., D.C.L., Professor of Greek in Harvard University. New Edition, revised and enlarged. 8vo. 14s.

A Greek Grammar. By the Same. Cr. 8vo. 6s.

A Greek Grammar for Schools. By the Same. Cr. 8vo. 3s 6d.

A Greek Grammar for Schools and Colleges. By James Hadley. Revised by F. de F. Allen. Cr. 8vo. 6s.

First Steps to Greek Prose Composition. By Blomfield Jackson, M.A. Pott 8vo. 1s 6d. KEY, for Teachers only. Pott 8vo. 3s 6d.

Second Steps to Greek Prose Composition, with Examination Papers. By the Same. Pott 8vo. 2s 6d. KEY, for Teachers only. Pott 8vo. 3s 6d.

Exercises in the Composition of Greek Iambic Verse. By Prof. H. Kynaston, D.D. With Vocabulary. Ex. fcap. 8vo. 5s. KEY, for Teachers only. Ex. fcap. 8vo. 4s 6d.

Parallel Passages for Translation into Greek and English. With Indexes. By Rev. E. C. Mackie, M.A. Gl. 8vo. 4s 6d.

Macmillan's Greek Course. Edited by Rev. W. G. Rutherford, M.A., LL.D., Headmaster of Westminster. Gl. 8vo.
FIRST GREEK GRAMMAR—ACCIDENCE. By the Editor. 2s.
FIRST GREEK GRAMMAR—SYNTAX. By the Same. 2s.
ACCIDENCE AND SYNTAX. In one Volume. 3s 6d.
EASY EXERCISES IN GREEK ACCIDENCE. By H. G. Underhill, M.A. 2s.
A SECOND GREEK EXERCISE BOOK. By Rev. W. A. Heard, M.A. 2s 6d.
EASY EXERCISES IN GREEK SYNTAX. By Rev. G. H. Nall, M.A. 2s 6d.

Macmillan's Greek Reader. Stories and Legends. A First Greek Reader, with Notes, Vocabulary, and Exercises. By F. H. Colson, M.A. Globe 8vo. 3s.

A Table of Irregular Greek Verbs, classified according to the arrangement of Curtius's Greek Grammar. By J. M. Marshall, M.A. 8vo. 1s.

First Greek Reader. By Prof. John E. B. Mayor, M.A. Fcap. 8vo. 4s 6d.

Greek for Beginners. By Rev. Prof. J. B. Mayor, M.A. Part I., with Vocabulary, 1s 6d. Parts II. and III., with Vocabulary and Index. Fcap. 8vo. 3s 6d. Complete in one Vol. 4s 6d.

The New Phrynichus: being a Revised Text of the Ecloga of the Grammarian Phrynichus. With Introduction and Commentary. By the Rev. W. G. Rutherford, M.A., LL.D. 8vo. 18s.

First Lessons in Greek. Adapted to Goodwin's Greek Grammar, and designed as an Introduction to the Anabasis of Xenophon. By J. W White. Cr. 8vo. 3s 6d.

Attic Primer. Arranged for the use of beginners. By J. Wright, M.A Extra fcap. 8vo. 2s 6d.

MACMILLAN AND CO., LONDON.

www.ingramcontent.com/pod-product-compliance
Lightning Source LLC
Chambersburg PA
CBHW030629270326
41927CB00007B/1364